"Above all, continue fiddling
whilst Rome is burning.
For fiddling is your nature.

.... And there never was a Rome."

-Edsel Terrick

Love Awakened

Love Awakened

A RELATIONSHIP PRIMER

by: EDSEL TERRICK

Library of Congress Control Number: 2019907865

PAPERBACK: 978-1-7333366-0-4
EBOOK: 978-1-7333366-1-1

Ordering Information:

For orders and inquiries, please contact:
1-888-404-1388
www.goldtouchpress.com
book.order@goldtouchpress.com

Printed in the United States of America

CONTENTS

I think you should
go home after work.
...You can make a
nice salad for dinner.
Maybe a cup of decaf tea?
...I know! You can put
on your favorite sappy
romantic comedy and
finish putting together
that "Tuscan Villa"
puzzle you've been
working on!

Put together a puzzle?!
Are you kidding me?! Why
don't you just save yourself
some time and pick up fifty
cats and a knitting set on
the way home!
NO WAY, SISTER!
What you are
going to do is let your
hair down, put on some
make-up, put on something
slutty, order a pitcher of
Margaritas, and have a
GOOD TIME for once!

ACKNOWLEDGMENTS

I would like to thanks and recognize the following people who were vital in the writing and production of this book:

- Mike Zug, illustrator and cartoonist extraordinaire, who so creatively, insightfully and playfully produced our cartoons.
- Kamonkwan Tongmusick, my intimate partner, who is often my support, cheerleader, playmate, partner-in-crime, and frequent hero.
- My wonderful daughters, Angelica, Sarah, Jazminh, and Jennifer Juniper, who continue to teach me about the value of being human.
- Joel Linnane, who presented himself as a follower, but was more often a courageous leader. May he rest in peace.
- All my friends and associates in recovery, who have loved and accepted me when I couldn't. When I was good—and when I was bad.
- My sons, Christopher and Shaun, who in spite of their pain while growing up, see some value in me as a friend.
- And mostly, to you dear reader, who honor me with your time and attention, and for a while allow me to be a teacher. You give me value, and reason.

Welcome Pilgrim!

You are already on the road to
peace and joy. Not created by your relationships,
but ENHANCED and deepened by them!

How do I know this?
In a way, you and I are alone here together.
We are intimately comparing our thoughts, ideas,
disappointments, distortions, and confusion.

Though it probably doesn't feel like it yet,
this is the beginning of a new relationship—
One where you know yourself as the actual source of your despair,
suffering, sorrow, disappointments and life frustrations.
You allow all this to be known not only to yourself,
but to your chosen partner.

You are working towards true intimacy.
A precious goal, and attainable.

Enjoy the journey.

INTRODUCTION

Is it possible to love deeply and be embraced by intimacy's arms without surrendering your values and truths? Can relationships continue to grow even when a partner wants to run out the back door, either emotionally or physically? Can a committed long-term relationship have a new beginning every day, every moment? Is it indeed possible that all relationships can be fluid and move to the "next level" (whatever that is!) on a daily basis?

In a word, YES!

The intention of this book is to empower you to have exceptional relationships and make your quality of life excellent. The secret to making this happen is waking up from the miasma of cultural romantic scripts that are believed, accepted as true, and acted out on every day.

Most of the fuel for current relationships is fear, not love. *Love Awakened!* moves you out of fear into a permanent space of love, respect, and acceptance. Actually, something that is already within you, and merely needs to be let out!

Try on this analogy for a moment. Most people breathe in a shallow, stressful pattern that barely gets air into their lungs. The result is a lack of oxygen to the brain so they walk around foggy and forgetful most of the time. If told to take a deep breath, most people suck air into their chest; whereas a truly deep breath is to breathe into their abdomen where the act of breathing has the most health benefit.

The metaphor: Most people live in a fearful, shallow space. The result is that they walk around in a media-induced fog about how love works and how to give and fully enjoy the experience of love.

The result of this shallowness and lack of awareness of one's own inner workings is repeated disappointments in love, and then disappointments in life. And a life lived without loving, is a life not fully lived.

Discard Shallow Solutions

Men, how many of you think Viagra will do it for you? Women, how many of you purchased Victoria Secret's push-up bras in the last twelve months, hoping for love?

This is all a dream. A lie that has been so deeply rooted in your mind that you believe that even love itself is a process of cause and effect. When, truly, it is NOT.

If I invite you to love more deeply, you'd say, "I already do," just like those who think a shallow breath means that they have a healthy breath until they keel over dead from lack of oxygen. Loving from a shallow space leaves you hungry for more love, and this "keep looking" message kicks in. So you continue to wonder why true love has eluded you.

Perhaps your perceptions of love have deluded you? Does understanding from where real love emanates remain a mystery?

Let's break through those misperceptions and delusions to the deepest form of intimacy. Through understanding and the application of a few of the principles contained herein, you can break all chains of failure, frustration and loss that people experience on a daily basis. Moreover, if you are diligent, your results will be that much better— guaranteed! And if it doesn't work, you can always go back to the same old same old . . .

So with an open heart, allow me to touch your mind, your imagination, and your spirit. We start this journey together.

To know truth, you must pass through, and understand accurately, your own experience. But chances are this experience is already recorded, but has never accurately viewed and interpreted. This is your chance.

Living THE DREAM!

I've seen so many people who have become captured in relationships and unwittingly surrender their true self in the process, as if this if "the cost of doing business". It is NOT.

Because of the very nature of the memory, and the workings of the mind, these patterns develop and are actually embraced without even knowing it! There is almost a severe spiritual surrender that occurs, often little by little, until the relationship, and even the self, are unrecognizable!

Patterns of fear and limitation and compromise sneak up on you. Life seems good and relationships appear smooth, and then "kaboom!" That nagging feeling hits you. The sense of incompleteness whispers incessantly, "something just isn't right in this relationship! It *must* be my partner!"

This intuitive scream causes you to pause and take stock. All the ingredients for intimacy seem to be in the right place. The fit seems perfect. You have made good decisions, and your life is unfolding, just as you envisioned! But it doesn't feel like you thought it would. What is amiss? What is the problem?

Know the feeling?

I've Been There!

A number of years ago, I was faced with this realization...

I'd met most of my life goals (ego-defined, of course), and I was progressing towards the others, or creating more as I prodded along. I was winding down and enjoying the apparent rewards of success and achievement. I was quite comfortable in my second marriage and thought it would last forever.

I sensed that this was "as good as it gets," and then suddenly realized that it wasn't enough! Where did THAT thought come from? What I thought would bring me a continuous and profound feeling of peace and completeness was leaving me empty and even ANGRY. I felt trapped and nothing made sense. Like most of you, I asked myself the same questions: "Where did I go wrong? When did I zig when I should have zagged?"

Then it happened—my quintessential cathartic out-of-body experience, which raised all the questions I am going to ask you in this book. Together, we will consider the truths of love. In chapter one, I'll share my soul-searing experience and we can compare notes on the right questions to ask to get the deeper answers.

Being captured and harmfully surrendering in love is not gender-based. It is a common human experience. This book says that if your life just doesn't feel right, and you aren't where you want to be at this very moment, it is difficult, but definitely worthwhile to examine your own truths and the foundation and dynamics of your relationships. Uncomfortable, yes! Beneficial, absolutely!

How to Read This Book

Slowly! And with a sense of humor! As you read this book, assume nothing. Always be prepared to discern, interpret, embrace or reject as you see fit. Take what seems appropriate and reasonable and try it! You might be pleasantly surprised by your results. Or shocked… but reap the benefits of the resultant changes anyway! You are not controlling that.

Please keep in mind that this book only contains recipes, not directives. And even the recipes are intended to assist in the preparation of the appetizers, and desserts, in the banquet known as intimate relationships. The main course is up to you! Your are encouraged to use your own creativity and awareness to design, prepare, and enjoy this wonderful meal!

And it might be a good idea to have a yellow (or green or purple) highlighter handy to focus on concepts that might be of particular interest or use to you. And, also, make this book virtually unsalable on EBay. So your friends and family can serendipitously discover this book, and understand where it all went wrong!!!!

If you feel uncomfortable or confused, then you are on the right track. I've used several tools in this book to wake up your mind and heart to your deeper truths: provocative thoughts, stories, humor, cartoons, spicy language, and straightforward conversation. I hope they do make you uncomfortable enough to search for deeper truths about love and intimacy, and about yourself. If you are in fact feeling that discomfort, you are getting my message, and that is of utmost importance for you.

Freedom, and even intimacy, in a relationship, requires letting go. It appears counter-intuitive. When freedom is surrendered as the price for intimacy, the price itself negates and destroys the intimacy. Grabbing, controlling, demanding and suffocating are the elements of destruction within a relationship. Need, desire, and passion associated with perceived self-fulfillment, though sounding romantic, are the very toxins that can destroy something of beauty and great value.

What is Romance?

Romantic love is very important, as it is one of the most intimate possible relationships, other than with one's own true self. It's a type of love that is a lot about oneness - two people becoming intimately connected to the point where the two is indistinguishable from the one. It's like a two-people system, a new thing that is the sum of its parts, but perhaps more than what was before. Imagine a bike with two wheels: the two wheels form a pair and together with the other parts of the bike they form a whole. Would you imagine a bike without wheels? What would be the point of the bike? What's a bike with one wheel, kind of pointless, no?

Now, this analogy is not entirely correct. Actually, the analogy is not correct at all... Although things seem to be so, and they are to some extent, most people get completely distracted by the awesome idea of the whole, they want to find that special someone that completes them. They miss the fact that they, as they are right now, are complete in and of itself! How Awesome is that?!

Finally, romantic love is beautiful and to some extent it is a game of becoming one, pretending to be one. A lot of people feel a tremendous rush to find their partners, to feel that completeness, and they think romantic love must be the ultimate key. But in fact it is just a game, and the most benefit from this game is extracted precisely when one is not completely reliant on the game, not completely immersed in it.

The Source of Deception

Forgive such a strong word as deception. But truly, you have received information about love and relationships that is not accurate. If you expect intimacy to look and feel like your favorite movie, you're in for quite a lot of disappointments. The same applies to life overall. Your efforts to create not only the background and characters, but to manage and dictate the process and outcome, is actually the source of the problem!

Realize as soon as you can muster the courage that disappointment is actually a good thing! The conflicts and successful resolutions in a relationship make you AND the relationship more vital, and is a wonderful foundation for long-term commitment and intimacy, both to yourself and to your partner.

In the first few chapters you will learn where much of that false information and romantic scripting came from. You'll be surprised at how much of your thoughts and expectations are tied into these messages.

Solutions

If we stopped at identifying the source of the problems and mistakes that people make in love, this would be only an interesting book about communication, human interaction, and relationships. We will go further. We will explore and recommend practical solutions to change your perceptions, your quality of life, and of course the genuineness of your love relationships.

We're embarking on an intimate journey, which is no small task. Our very selves are defined, reflected and validated by the nature and dynamics of our relationships. There are none so fraught with error and benefits than these relationships.

Accepting that intimate relationships are tremendously instrumental in living a fulfilled and purposeful life, what are the possibilities?

- Can I become fully involved, committed, and still maintain my autonomy and personal freedom?
- Can I approach a relationship differently, and not surrender vital parts of myself in the process?
- What are those vital parts that need to be acknowledged and preserved?
- Can I avoid capturing and being captured?
- And have a truly deep, long-lasting and meaningful relationship?

You are asking for truth, but you are merely seeking comfort, and reinforcement. And to create further distress, you demand permanence and completeness in the answer, as you do in your relationships. That demand in itself annihilates true benefit, and affection.

This book is not meant to give you a new answer or answers. But only to awaken you to the fact that you already have the answers... But have overlooked or ignored them.

Well, fellow traveler, you now know the purpose of this book: to ask NEW questions about relationships that you didn't even know could be asked. And then get the practical answers on how to find and experience the closest intimacy beyond your wildest dreams! And it will be your real self who loves and is subsequently loved. All without effort. Now, THAT IS as good as it gets!

INTIMACY

Chapter 1

Genuine Love

***Entering and Maintaining a relationship based on who we are,
rather than who someone wants us to be,
or even who WE want to be!***

My Wake-up Call

The following experience was instrumental in changing the course of my life so drastically that it was threatening and horrifying to everyone around me. They thought I had taken leave of my senses—which I probably had.

Marie Jo was my wife, business partner, confidante and most everything else for the sixteen years of our marriage. I confess, for a while I even considered her my "other half" (shame on me!). We were a wonderful match in the fulfilling years of our marriage. Then I had one of those defining moments of awareness that altered the course of my life and hers.

Numbed Out

Marie Jo and I had completed an exhaustive shopping experience at Stop and Shop in York, Pennsylvania. We strutted toward our gleaming Mercedes SUV with two brimming carts of groceries. We were among the many middle-aged people living a life of excess and feeling very comfortable doing it. "Reaping what we had sown", we had both worked hard, and this was apparently one of the benefits. But was it?

The nearly full moon glowed on this summer evening at 7:30 PM. We continued pushing our grocery carts to our car that was about one hundred yards away, and she was talking at me.

I must confess that I have no idea what she was telling me. By that point we had been together sixteen years, and there was so little diversity or change in our relationship and perspectives, that no doubt what she was saying had been said many times before. So I naturally and comfortably tuned her out. I had created and reinforced a pattern and paradigm so strongly that it left no room for creativity or excitement.

Suddenly, without reason, I stopped walking. Marie Jo didn't notice, and kept pushing her cart. Amazingly and predictably she continued talking, not even noticing that I wasn't there. She continued her monologue until she reached the car.

In the Blink of an Eye

At that moment, I had a significant "out of body experience." A sudden awareness. An epiphany. Having been drug and alcohol free for a number of years, I couldn't blame this experience on being stoned!

Floating above myself, I literally saw myself standing in the parking lot in York, Pennsylvania brimming over with my own demands and desires! I saw Marie Jo continue talking at me. I saw the carts full of groceries and it seemed peculiar, unsettling and surreal. People scurrying around doing what suddenly seemed like meaningless and pointless things, only based on self-interest and self-gratification! And I was one of them. Yipes!

The Cosmic Question

As I fully experienced this vision, a cosmic question entered my mind. This is a question that was unexpected, but totally relevant: *"Edsel, if you could place yourself anywhere in this world, with anybody to be attached to and in a relationship with, would that truly complete you, and make give your life meaning?* The answer was a categorical "NO"! And, in that instant, I realized that I was looking on the outside for something I foolishly believed was necessary on the inside! In other words, given the clear choice, would I be doing exactly what I was doing at this particular moment if not for the demands and directives of my ravenously hungry mind and delusions of need for pleasure and satisfaction?

I was stunned to hear an answer echoing from the core my being. "No." was the profound answer, with no equivocation. Not only was I running in the wrong race, I was chasing the wrong rabbit *(or rather, realized that no rabbit needed to be caught)*!!!

These twenty seconds felt like an eternity. Finally, after Marie Jo opened the car trunk and started loading groceries, she realized that I wasn't there with her, listening to her story.

"Edsel, what's wrong?"

"Everything is wrong, especially with me." I responded.

"What do you mean, Edsel?"

"Marie Jo, everything here is wrong; there is nothing right here. I have been and continue being driven by needs and demands that are self-generated, created, and subsequently totally unimportant and unreal." Of course, she had absolutely NO CLUE!!!

What's Crucial?

I was totally unprepared and confused by my thoughts and feelings. And MJ was even more so, of course. But I instinctively knew that I had discovered something vitally important to me, and I needed to hold onto it.

"It is critical that I don't let this go. What's crucial is that my life and experiences have taken me to exactly where I am, and I don't want to be here, and I don't want to continue being with you merely to create feelings of security and value in myself." I blurted out, shamefully.

"Wow, are you having a bad day or something?" MJ asks kindly. "Did I do something wrong?'

"I know what I'm saying doesn't make any sense at all. I have to think about it some more, but I know that this is not the life I would be living if I was not actually living a dream. You know, Marie Jo, both you and I have the choice, and a responsibility."

We went to intensive counseling, and tried and tried to undo the damage that was done by not being aware and awake, and therefore genuine, with each other. But we were now total strangers, and we were unable to reclaim what was lost or deeply buried . . . . our true selves.

"Reward" is the ultimate soil of the mind. Even in relationship, it discerns and determines what the rewards are from a perspective of self. If rewards cannot be identified and sufficiently tallied, the mind assumes that the relationship is not beneficial, and should be terminated. Mostly in the expectation and anticipation of finding a partner that will FINALLY meet the incessant and imaginary demands of the self.

By NOT being honest, and allowing myself to be enslaved by my demanding and hungry mind, I had inadvertently, but severely, diminished the quality of our relationship. By not being ME (whoever that really was), I was taking something extremely valuable from my wonderful wife! And I had to change it . . . . That was the beginning of the end of my relationship with Marie Jo. Six months from that day we were officially separated and we were moving smartly towards a divorce. Subsequently, Marie Jo became my ex-wife, and, naturally, my best friend.

Making Drastic Changes

I changed my life: where I was, whom I was with, and how I was doing things. Or more accurately I changed my perspective, and began looking at myself, my own greeds and imaginary needs, rather than being pulled along by them.

Even my values and goals seemed to change instantaneously. But in fact, nothing needed to be changed. It was the exact opposite. I needed to acknowledge, and have the courage to be, who I truly was. Please, dear reader, know . . . . this is one of the most difficult things in life to do!!! A fine madness, but quite scary!

In hindsight, and in mentoring others through similar life experiences, my take on this whole thing is that there was really no shift; no *sudden* shift, anyway. More likely, I had started changing, or rather acknowledging my perceptions years before, and was unable or unwilling to accept and admit it. Even more likely, I had needs and desires that I never knew about, and was being constantly directed by this crowd of bullies! A man in his mid-forties! Feeling and acting like a teenager! Sound familiar?

> *"The only charm of marriage is that it makes a life of deception necessary for both parties"*
>
> —Oscar Wilde

Fear of Change

I had somehow known that aspects of my life were wrong, or at least, not right according to my true nature *(of course, STILL not knowing what that was!)*. However, I lacked the courage or the personal commitment and responsibility to do anything about it. Fear of change was a limiting force, more than I cared to admit.

I could not acknowledge that the life I was living, the person I was, the woman I was married to, and many of what seemed to be natural and beneficial choices I'd made (or didn't make) were neither adequate nor reflective of my who I truly was. I held myself captive to a fantasy for years, and now I felt totally alone, but finally myself. A worthy trade!

Over time, I've observed that many people go through similar feelings, and this book is a result of my desire to move you, dear reader, from captivity to freedom within your intimate relationships, both with others and with your self. I will explain to you how to have true intimacy without "drinking the cool aid", or imprisoning yourself in the proverbial "Matrix". I will give you a clue even at this early stage—the captor is, and has always been, you!

> *He valued emotion—not for itself, but because it is the only final path to intimacy.*
>
> —Edward Morgan Forster

Your Wake Up Call

In the mentoring and counseling that I do, fitness training and through other groups of people looking for life-improvement through self-discovery, I often see them walking around, muttering quietly, "Feed me," knowing that they are unfulfilled. They look spiritually hungry and intellectually under-challenged. Their heads are down, their emotions numb. They also sense that something is missing, but can't quite figure out what was lost.

Human relationship cannot be controlled or planned. Either it is natural, or contrived. If natural, it will grow and blossom effortlessly. Or it WON'T! If contrived, it will ALWAYS remain a burden, and a source of sorrow, despair and suffering.

The giving up is the first step to true intimacy. The magic is in realizing that there is nothing to give up. For nothing, and nobody, is owned. That illusion of ownership, and subsequent attempts to control another person, is a certain path to despair and suffering. And, in this vicious path, the other person is almost always blamed for the poison that actually comes from the professed "lover ".

> *"Do not go gentle into that good night.*
> *Rage, rage against the dying of the light."*
>
> —Dylan Thomas,
> *Do Not Go Gentle into that Good Night*

Dylan Thomas talks about raging against the dark night of death; he alludes to *not* living quiet desperate lives, captured and unknowing. The wake-up call hasn't yet unleashed the freedom-seeker, the wild one, the rebel, the knower. The restless one, waiting to be freed!

Have you ever imagined a ferocious and untamed animal within yourself growling, yelling, jumping and kicking to break through your miasma? Yet, on the outside, you maintain a calm, unanimated freeze.

Your untamed animal wants to come out, play and yell and scream. Can it climb to the surface of your consciousness, and beyond even to your very awareness?

Death of the created self is essential to intimacy. Without death of the parts, no union can truly happen. There would be a combining of stories, faces, memories, personalities, desires, beliefs and faces. But in this realm, no true union is feasible. By their very separate existence, if perceived thusly, an impenetrable wall always remains. Ignoring the wall is what we have trained ourselves to do. Acknowledging the wall in fact is in fact the vital first step in eliminating it. It is merely another creation that grows out of our individual fear, and need to be supreme and permanently separate.

Leap-Free Quiz

1. What is your wild, untamed animal inside?
2. Does it feel emotionally and spiritually starved?
3. Is it intellectually hungry?
4. Spiritually muffled?
5. Are you willing to let the wild animal express?

Beware! Once you discover your true nature and your real passions, it is difficult, if not impossible, to go back! They'll never again fit in a box or be satisfied with a convenient and placating label

Leap Free

There's a joyous human being inside you, and an amazing spirit attached to it, trying to get out. Locked in by ideas of limitation, a bruised ego from the past, or lack of self-confidence, and haunting stories from your mind's memory, this energy is suffocated. Imagine totally un-restraining the captured one and admonishing, "Go, dance and make merriment." What glorious freedom!

Read on—that freedom is yours.

Struggling for Your Freedom

Each of us recognizes when something isn't right with us, within us or our relationships. For a while, you might distract yourself with CNN, or "I Love Lucy." Perhaps a few rounds of golf or a hot bubble bath relaxes the discomfort in your gut momentarily. You sufficiently distract yourself from truth, which temporarily lets you off the hook. It's a shame. We like to keep up appearances far beyond the time that the deeper reality starts pulling at us.

Moments of Choice

Don't push away such feelings as "sensed it, a hit to the gut, jerked around, or creeping thoughts" because they might very well be clarity. Recognize them. I believe that everyone has these moments when we recognize the deeper truth lurking within, but few choose to acknowledge or act on them.

Yet, the deeper truths of these feelings don't go away and will keep nagging the one who wants to experience freedom, truth or new insight. That's you, oh drowning one. Come on up for a breath of fresh air!

We are given ample opportunities to face our feelings and ourselves. A lot of people wait for a near-death experience or some catastrophe. Suddenly their perceptions shift and their priorities change. Unexpectedly, life itself becomes more precious; everyday seems as the potential "final day." As a result, people make abrupt shifts.

Can Changes Be Made without Crises?

Selfishness is routed in the mistaken ideas of oneself... And can only be changed when these ideas are clearly perceived as false. One's garden must have the necessary elements that are necessary to support such a transmutation. And the preparation itself comes from the awareness and the responsibility of focus.

Imagine if you could make these shifts without calamity, without experiencing a significant loss in health, relationships or occupations.

Consider that you could make changes by mere choice.

Hoo-hah. Freedom, here I am!

Embrace this concept. Grab onto it, and give it value. Let it be a motivator for change, for improvement.

You can voluntarily seize the moment and take the first step out of captivity!

They made an engaging-looking couple in the swank restaurant:
The man was handsome, graying and obviously well off;
the woman was a joy to any eye—
very young, ravishing and delectable.
As they each read their menus, the gentleman asked his date
what she would like to eat.
She scanned the menu yet again, and said, "To begin, I'll have
two champagne cocktails, then a dozen oysters on the half shell
and a tureen of turtle soup.
As entrees I'll have the filet of English sole followed by pheasant
under glass, plus an a la carte order of asparagus tips.
For dessert, they may just bring the cart.
Somewhat surprised not only by her appetite, but by the cost of all
of this, he asked, "Tell me. Do you eat this well at home too?"
"Well, no . . ." she admitted,
"But no one at home wants to sleep with me either."

Distractions or Clarity

Our attention and focus is controlled by needs, challenges and threats, because life is filled with distractions and many too many silly stories. Without warning or reason, at some point in your life, those distractions momentarily cease and then you recognize truth. You can see clearly in that moment. Through the piercing of the veil, you unmistakably know the flaw in *your* life. You sense it. You cannot deny it. Somehow you know it.

With the concept of "relationship" come expectations, memories of past relationships, and further personally and culturally conditioned mental concepts of what a "relationship" should be like. Then I would try to make reality conform to these concepts. And it never does. And again I suffer. The fact of the matter is: there are no relationships. There is only the present moment, and in the moment there is only relating.

We're faced with the realization of our selfish decisions, our mortality, lost dreams or inadequate life preparation and celebration.

More than anything, we have to admit that we're ultimately responsible for the quality and value of our own lives. We are not leaves blowing in the wind. We are responsible for who and what and where we are, and how our life is playing out. If you follow this line of awareness, we are even responsible for the world we create around us!

Seeing Clearly

This kind of eye-opener is like being on a trip with a clear set of directions. You have a map and it tells you exactly what road you should be traveling. Then out of the blue you feel queasy and know that you are not in the right place.

o   Your knowing defies your logic.
o   Worse, you realize you're *not* headed to the place that is most beneficial to you, and alignment with your true nature.
o   Moreover, you're not even sure of your destination anymore and you start questioning the journey itself. That's perfect!

I assure you that people of all ages have these wake-up calls. "Hey you, imprisoned one, wake-up! The prison door is open."

Wake-up calls are opportunities to re-examine and review, and then take personal responsibility for the very fabric of your life.

> *My belief is that personal freedom cannot grow*
> *beyond personal responsibility. The more people*
> *that learn to be fully accountable for their lives,*
> *the more freedom each of us can enjoy and*
> *the more fulfilling all of our lives will be.*
>
> —Reed Konsler

Just Another Story

Jill's moment of clear sight happened about six months into her marriage to her doctoral professor, Leonard. Their dating evolution was classic: a whirlwind courtship of romance, long conversations over wine, lingering sunsets, weekends hiking and sharing childhood memories. They discussed the mistakes of their previous marriages over expensive dinners. Life felt so good, they were certain that they were a cosmic match.

They married.

Over the next several months, Jill discovered that her new husband didn't want any children, and she'd dreamed of having a house-full. To make matters worse, Leonard had a new book deadline for his publisher and spent weekends writing. Jill felt alone. Jill was alone!

No problem, she thought. Life happens and we'll adjust, and eventually he'll change his mind. But he didn't. Jill started getting headaches and asked herself continually, "What am I doing wrong? Am I too young for him? Where did the romance go?"

One morning, as they both left for work, Leonard planted the customary kiss on Jill's cheek, got in his car and drove to the university. Jill collapsed into tears against the side of her car, realizing that she created so many unsupported expectations about her marriage. The REAL Jill and Leonard never really met!

Mental Paradigms Beliefs, and Demands ARE Prisons!

Jill's mind created a fantasy marriage consisting of the ever-attentive, nurturing and affectionate husband. Leonard created a picture of the understanding wife who let him work and kept herself busy presumably making his life happy and comfortable. Each felt their reality was valid, and each was naturally disappointed.

We can learn a lot from this. Like Jill and Leonard, we create a story around a relationship in order to give it validity and what seems to be purpose. We then believe these pictures in our head. The mind habitually creates limitations and definitions of events, mostly filled with false meaning—all of which become our scripts for intimacy.

Knowing the Problem vs. Finding the Solution

These fantasies are real to us, and in fact, become our prison. Our mind convinces us that thoughts are the substance of your relationship. This is not true. Read that most important statement again to insure you get this ticket to the freedom train. **Thoughts and beliefs are NOT the substance of your relationship.**

When you are captured and the romantic notions don't play out the way you expect, you naturally blame whoever you're with. However, if you dump this partner, you'll find another with the same "faults" because you have the same pictures in your head. No one wants to repeat this pattern, right? Read on, and I'll show you how find the true happiness you desire in love. You deserve it! And you can have it!

A husband and wife were involved in a petty argument, both of them unwilling to admit they might be in error.
"I'll admit I'm wrong," the wife told her husband in a conciliatory attempt, "if you'll admit I'm right."
He agreed and, like a gentleman, insisted she go first.
"I'm wrong," she said.
With a twinkle in his eye, he responded, "You're right!"

Afterglow—Points to Ponder, and Remember

- o Each of us has a choice about how we choose to live life, and we are responsible for our choices (or lack of) and their outcomes.
- o Start with a serious look at how the fear of change may be running your life or keeping you from making the changes you need to make.
- o Discern whether you are a captive of a fantasy that hides the true self.
- o Everyone has moments of clarity when we recognize the deeper truth lurking within, but few of us choose to acknowledge or act on them.
- o Are you willing, in this moment, to choose freedom?
- o Our attention and focus are controlled by imagined needs, challenges, and threats because life is filled with distractions and many too many silly stories.
- o Mostly, we have to admit that we're ultimately responsible for the quality and value of our own lives.
- o **Thoughts are NOT the substance** of your relationship
- o Wake-up calls are opportunities to re-examine and review, and then take responsibility through different choices.

Don't forget to do the dishes
Can you take me to soccer practice?
Take me for a walk NOW, or I poop on the oriental...
BOW-WOW

Chapter 2

The A-B-C's of a Good Relationship

The need for intimacy in a relationship.

Getting Ready to "Fly Like an Eagle!"

Steps to Freedom

Realizing your mistakes (or rather your mind and ego centered demands and expectations) is the first step to freedom and trust in relationships. Being willing to be aware if these "tricks of the mind," and a willingness to change them (or more likely ignore them!) is the second step. Here's how:

Assessment and re-examination of where we are in our lives always has value. As Socrates so aptly put it, "The unexamined life is not worth living". An assessment might affirm that your relationship is already as good as it gets. If nothing else, it tells you "Yeah, yeah, this is great. This is where I want to be."

Unfortunately, my experience reveals that when most people truly examine and re-examine the quality of their relationships in reality's harsh light, they don't like what they see, and typically start to blame the other person or external circumstances for the apparent "deficiency".

Not liking the real picture is a wonderful moment! It is a circle of confusion, despair and clarity all mixed up together. The next step after confusion is often clarity.

> *Difficulties are meant to rouse, not discourage.*
> *The human spirit is to grow strong by conflict.*
>
> —William Ellery Channing

When we find something wrong in our relationship and keep our focus within, we may see a marriage counselor to get it fixed. More likely we will be provided with another "story" and directions on how to be more reasonable and acceptable. But being reasonable and acceptable is not the answer. Being real is!

Maybe you need a life review or to take time to re-examine your needs and expectations that are responsible for your partnership choices.

"Oh no!" you say. "I can't do that. It poses the possibility of dramatic change—I'm uncomfortable with that—hey, things could be worse—so I'll settle for mediocre. Thanks anyway."

Many people work from this standard of mediocrity. Don't you do it!

> *Happy marriages begin when we marry the ones we love, and they*
> *blossom when we love the ones we marry.*
>
> —Tom Mullen, *A Very Good Marriage*

Decline "OK", Go for Great!

Every human being deserves more than mediocre. You deserve the chance for celebration and periods of pure joy and complete fulfillment, even if transient. It is actually the realization of failure and despair that creates new impetus and opportunity. The process is that you don't suddenly see the truth. Rather, you recognize what is *not* the truth. It is the "Ah Ha" moment—the third step to freedom—recognizing untruths.

A quick summary of the three steps to freedom in relationships:

1. Realizing your mistaken judgments and criticisms.
2. Be open minded and willing to let them go.
3. Recognizing what is not YOUR truth.

Story Lines for Intimacy

A major problem is that the standard story lines for intimacy are faulty or totally in error: *Love will last forever. Love means (s)he'll never leave me. (S)he'll always agree with me, be loyal to me, think like I think, be romantic every day, will remember my birthday every year, validate my perceptions, do what I want to do, won't love anyone else but me, will fulfill my every desire, will be my only sex partner,* and so on, ad nauseum.

Quiz: What does your storyline for intimacy look like?

Answer the following true or false questions.
My story line for intimacy is:

Never having to say "I'm sorry." My partner will get it.
My partner has an obligation to stay with me no matter what I do.
Two partners in love will examine their attitude and perspective to allow movement with each other.
We belong to each other now—and forever.
My partner will always want what I want.
A constant feeling of love is the most important ingredient in the partnership.
My partner should take whatever I dish out.
Intimacy is based on honesty, friendship, respect and commitment.

So how did you do? If you answered "true" to the last one, and "somewhat" to the third one, then you are awake and have the open mind needed to consider ways to improve your relationships. If you answered true to any of the other questions, then, pilgrim, you're in good company.

Let's consider the ways that one gets captured in a relationship. Are you prepared to discover how you surrender and don't even know it? Open your eyes wide. Truth is at hand!

> *Relationship requires understanding and compassion.*
> *The constant need of forgiveness to a partner indicates a flaw in perception, and a red-flag indicating extreme self-centeredness and unabashed greed.*
>
> -Edsel Terrick

Ways to Get Captured

So many people are groping—almost drowning—while looking for a story of how intimacy should be. They're grabbing soap-opera scripts, comedy routines and faked reality scripts trying to make them fit into their nature and their situation. That just doesn't work.

How many of us watch situation comedies, then turn off the television and find we're in the same situation. The shows seemed funny at the time, but things are happening to us for real, they don't seem so funny anymore. How many have you said, "My life is like a soap opera."

We can't take another story and make it our own, no matter how hard we try.

Here are some typical styles in relationships:

o Easygoing-people take things as they come and have no idea what they want, need, or value, and so have no standards for intimacy in relationships. They're merely sharing space.
o Sponge-people absorb everything around them and try to live out multiple scripts, eventually becoming confused about what is real and lasting, overloaded, violated and uninspired.
o Chameleon-people become whoever they need to be for their partners, losing self in the process.

o This-way-only-people have such strong story lines that they spend their time trying to fit the pictures in their head. They have fixed ideas about what their lives should look like, what their partners should say, where they should live, and so on. Their true feelings are unexpressed and they feel shallow. Apparently powerful, but pitifully pathetic.

One Friday afternoon, two secretaries were hanging around the water cooler at the office. "Veronica, I just don't know what to do," Gloria said to her friend at work.
"That good-looking Alex in Accounting asked me out on a date for Saturday night. Should I go?"
"Oh, my God!" her friend exclaimed.
"He'll wine you, dine you, and then use any ruse to get you up to his apartment.
Then he'll rip off your dress and you'll have fantastic sex!"
"What should I do?" asked Gloria.
Her friend quickly replied, "Wear an old dress."

—Auntie M's Jokes, auntm.tripod.com

Prisoners of Love

To know true intimacy without feeling trapped or captured, requires that you ask yourself provoking questions and dig deeply for the most honest answers. So, grab a shovel!

o Can you accept love without giving up your personal freedom?
o Do you recognize feeling trapped in a relationship, and understand exactly WHERE that feeling comes from?
o Does love imply or require that a partner be a possession?
o Can the ritual of courtship be improved or even discarded?
o Can we find someone to complete us?
o Then again, should we seek completion through another?

These questions may bring forth your memories of the feeling of failure and the fear of repeating the same relationship mistakes. But, dear pilgrim, remember that nothing is a mistake unless repeated!

We continually use our memories of past failure, and the events that led up to it, as vital information to prevent future "failure." *How presumptuous* that is! We are looking in the wrong place! It is our own selves that need to be examined, and embraced.

> *A person's value in relationships is not based on talents, triumphs, successes, their knowledge and/or abilities—or even their willingness to learn more. It is more likely their willingness to be truly honest in that relationship, coupled with their ability to do just that! Of course, if one isn't honest with themselves, honesty with another becomes truly impossible.*
>
> —Edsel Terrick

How We Order Our World

- People develop standards of behavior in relationships based on others' needs and wishes, not on their own needs, style and very nature.
- We choose relationships based on the experiences, advice, and *limitations* of others, not from our own inner urgings and creative abilities.
- We tend to believe that if we feel "good" (good being subjective) being with a person, then this warrants attachment to them. "Good" can be happy, content, comfortable or whatever kind of feelings you want to put in that box.

We often believe that such an emotional reaction has strong validity for determining whether there is value in continuing that relationship. If someone makes us feel good, does that mean that the person is really good for us? Remember please! The feeling is from YOU, not from them. You are merely giving them either credit or blame for it.

If a relationship gives us a sense of comfort, continuity, acceptance and all the wonderful feelings that are supposed to go with it, does that necessarily indicate that the relationship is nurturing, that it supports and enhances personal growth?

Common Traps of Deception

If you're anything like me, you can come up with a variety of creative rationalizations and justifications for almost any behavior, thought, belief, or subsequent emotional reaction ranging from the subtly inappropriate to the outrageously destructive. So, with that in mind, here are some of the more common traps that people fall (or spring) into that diminish the quality of their relationships, and consequently their lives.

Trap #1—Chasing "Good" Feelings

- o   Feeling good or comfortable or content with another person may very well be feel real. However, it doesn't necessarily indicate that the relationship is allowing and promoting personal growth and true intimacy.
- o   True intimacy acknowledges our individuality and differences
- o   It promotes a level of honesty and interaction that makes the relationship more meaningful as time passes. NOT more compliant and structured.

Relationships should take you beyond the good feelings. Feelings are not an indicator of value because we respond emotionally, based on earlier experiences (emotional memory), and we can so easily trap ourselves if our primitive feeling indicator says, "Grab that one. Feels good. Good catch." Captured!

Trap #2—New Experience/Old Feeling

Often there is *one* significant feeling that we derive initially from a relationship. This is often comfort, value, uniqueness, nurturing or perhaps belonging. This feeling is important, but often one-dimensional. It is self-created, and is temporary.

That good feeling is great, but it is not nearly enough to make the relationship mature and fully satisfying. This is the trap and pitfall of emotional recall.

Don't Settle for the Appetizer!

That good feeling that you had in your relationship was just an appetizer. For an infant, feeling nurtured would be totally complete. Add a feeling of safety to that, and you have one happy baby!

But we're adults, and we need a whole rich buffet. We need more than the good feeling for true intimacy. The appetizer tastes good, but we're only satisfied with the appetizer because we know that dinner is coming. We don't diminish the appetizer, but why not go for the full meal, and you can have dessert too. It's an all-you-can-eat buffet. Why not truly indulge?

Feeling Principles

- Put emotional events and emotional responses to people and situations in perspective, and understand that it is YOU that creates and categorizes the feelings, NOT the other person.
- Don't negate them or minimize them. Just acknowledge them.
- Don't throw feelings away and pretend they have no meaning. They do have meaning for you. Your job is to discern the meaning of your emotions clearly from your own truth and separate truth from "scripts" that are in your head. They are the clues that let you know who you truly are, and what you truly value.

Past feelings are not the rulers that you use to determine whether you're headed into an intimate relationship. It *is* important to know how you feel, but it is equally important to put it all in perspective. So if we can't use feeling good with someone to be an indicator of the relationship value, then what indicator do we use?

The answer is usually a willingness to "suffer" through not only what are normally described or interpreted as "good" feelings, but to accept, honor and even welcome feelings that are not typically considered good.

It is imperative in this domain that you understand that your suffering is self-created, typically based on the unwillingness to adjust to either the world as you perceive it, or to yourself.

Trap #3—Feeling Sad Means Something Bad

How many times in your relationship have you felt unloved, unprotected, or unappreciated? When you feel bad, does your brain burn this message into your mind: *The relationship is no good. You have to get out or make a change now.*

Whoa, that little devil voice convinces you that only good feelings equate to a good relationship. What rubbish! Do your emotional memories mean that the relationship is no good? Does that mean that we need to do something to change it, or even that something needs to be changed?

NO! The feeling is your personal wake-up call. Remember in Chapter One, we discussed the value of waking up to the deeper nagging truths within you? It's a signpost that says, "Hey, you are not getting the real message here." Typically you make the assumption that the problem is with your partner.

"If only she would understand me!"

"If only he would appreciate me more, listen with love; desire me the right way; say the right thing; or dance the right dance."

You run the "If Only" trap. Ta Da!—captured by the wishful thinker in a prison of false expectations.

Pop Quiz
(Let's see if you've been paying attention!)

You realize quite definitely that you're very angry at your partner for not hugging you when you felt lonely and needy this morning. You should:

A. Have a temper tantrum until you get the love and nurturing that you rightfully deserve.

B. Mourn and lament the incident, and finally become convinced that you made a lousy choice and your partner just can't fill your emotional needs, and dump him/her.

C. Acknowledge that your partner is incapable of true intimacy, and find a lover who is.

D. At an appropriate time, let your partner know how you felt, and what your perceived needs are. Be known.

E. Refuse to answer the question now, because you know that by the time you finish this book, you'll REALLY know the answer.

Go ahead and choose E. It does make the most sense at this stage of learning. Let's not get ahead of ourselves, now!!!

Trap #4—The Rescuer

It is amazing how we often repeat the same actions, and expect different results (the definition of insanity)!

I've heard so many women (and quite a few men when they're honest) complain about always ending up with "losers." This is no accident. There is a reason—a very subtle need, but one that is tremendously damaging. Forgive the expression, but you are a Rescuer!

A Rescuer believes that they have the power to fix or change another person. Do you have the absurd notion of "loving" someone back to health or sanity? The world is full of people who over-estimate their power, thus making a continuous stream of bad decisions not only for themselves, but often for the person they want to "fix".

Trap #5—Mind Games

The "If Only" game gets worse. Next you start envisioning how life would be different with someone else. This is a wonderfully creative and exciting cognitive, imaginative and emotional experience. You're developing a relationship with someone you haven't even met yet except based on the elements of the ideal in your thoughts. You're having sex with them, moving in, getting married, having babies and living happily ever after.

People play this mental game often. Why? Listen up—this is important. What they are saying and the message that they're telling themselves is, "The person I'm with now has failed me. There's got to be someone better, more appropriate, more loving, more understanding. So what I really need to do is dump this person. Get rid of him or her. Get them out of my life and start over again."

This might very well be true. This might be what needs to be done. But usually it is not. Instead, proceed with caution and easy does it.

o   Slow down
o   Stop pointing the finger, looking at the other person and start looking at yourself.
o   Take an honest look at where you are at and what deeper messages keep calling to you.
o   Be honest about what you really want and <u>need</u>. Sometimes these two things are difficult to sort out!

Maybe your awareness of who you are and what you focus on is different than before. Maybe when you were twenty-five you were focusing on the importance of choosing someone who would be a wonderful mother. Now you're fifty-something years old and you think a wonderful mom is good, but a great sex partner and adventurous spirit would even be better. Better yet, how about *both*!

Perceived needs change as life happens, and our priorities and focus change with them. To some degree, what you think you need is what you always could have believed you needed, but it just wasn't that important to you; or you didn't target it back then. You didn't change. The other person probably didn't change. Everything is the same; it's just that the picture looks different now because your mind has changed, and is merely creating new demands and expectations.

The important point here is to be cautious because you don't know what the cure is unless you're really accurate as to what the problem is.

We tend to look at the other person as a problem. Is that assumption fair? No, I would say it is not fair. It's not only unfair to the other person; I think it is unfair to us. It eliminates responsibility and the potential for change.

How we relate, or rather how well we love, depends on how empty we are of ideas, concepts, expectations.

In real love, there is not even one. How could there possibly be two. It is all a dream, an illusion. Not dangerous by nature, not even wrong, just imaginary and empty. A blown up balloon that appears monumental, but is merely emptiness surrounded by a thin restraint. Distracting surely, but lacking in relevance and real substance.

In Summary

We smugly weave deceit and failure into our endeavors by allowing what seems to be good sense and wisdom to sway us from our true path. We base our relationships from scripts that play on like movies in our minds. We continually employ memories of past apparent failure to deal with our future events, as if we could truly avoid disappointments.

Because we perceive our relationships through the lens of emotional memories, we trap ourselves in the past and doom ourselves to repeat the same events. Emotional recall often blocks or prevents genuine growth and interaction.

Often we are replaying an old drama with a new cast. In other words, we leave one relationship only to end up with the same feelings and problems in a new one. How can this happen? Don't we learn a lesson?

No, we don't. The fact is that we create these feelings and problems. Imprisoned by the past and doomed to capture. However there is hope, always ways to learn.

Allegory 101

Your foundation is faulty. You wreck the house because you know it has deteriorated, but the real problem is with the very foundation. However, you maintain the same one, and build another house on top of it. The new house looks great, but because you have a faulty foundation, the house starts sagging again.

"Gee," you think, "Obviously I'm not good at building houses. Maybe I need some help building houses. Maybe I'll get on the Internet. Maybe I'll get an astrologer. Maybe I'll find some computer program so I can build the right house"

You are totally trapped, and captured! You have never understood true intimacy. But soon you shall. Get ready to sing and dance and hot-cha-cha!

Afterglow—Points to Remember

- o Realizing your perceived mistakes is the first step to freedom in relationships. Being open-minded and willing to change your perspective is the second step.
- o When you are confused, the next step after confusion is clarity.
- o The wake-up journey is that you don't suddenly see the truth. Rather, you recognize what is *not* the truth. It is the "ah ha" moment—the third step to freedom—recognizing untruths.
- o We continually use our memories of past failure, and the events that led up to it, as vital information to prevent future "failure."
- o If someone makes us feel good, does that mean that the person is good for us?
- o Your job is to discern the meaning of your emotions clearly from your truth and separate truth from the contrived and meaningless "scripts" that play out in your head.

THOU SHALT NOT TALK ABOUT SEX
MY BIG BUTT IS STRICTLY OFF - TOPIC!
THERE WILL BE NO FRANK DISCUSSION OF ORGASM
PLEASE DO NOT MENTION MASTURBATION
IF I THINK IT'S "ICKY" - IT'S NOT HAPPENING!
Please be honest with me honey.
DON'T SCRATCH THAT ITCH!
KEEP YOUR FANTASIES TO YOURSELF
MMPPHhh!...
DO NOT MENTION PAST SEXUAL EXPERIENCES

Honesty . . . The Core of a Good Relationship

*Acknowledging and respecting ourselves
is the key to respecting others.*

> *There is only one thing more powerful than all the armies of the
> world, that is an idea whose time has come.*
>
> —Victor Hugo

Co-starring in Someone Else's Love Story

From chapter two, you now know that most of us have unrealistic pictures and expectations about love. Every day we encounter opportunities to surrender ourselves to these deceptions. We are busy capturing others because we are caught in the web of romantic myths. Emotional memories wrote our love stories and relationship scripts. Most of the time, we are successful in finding the co-star for our intimacy production. How do we derive these emotional scripts that compel us to live them out?

Did you identify with Scarlett's romantic manipulation of Rhett Butler, and his cavalier "Frankly, my dear, I don't give a damn?" Perhaps *Love Story* confused your heart into believing that love and suffering mean commitment. Have you held out for the princely hand that places Cinderella's glass slipper on your foot? Do Botox, silicone breasts, wonder bras, or Viagra keep your romance alive?

Do you relate to any of these?

Someday my prince will come	The Cinderella Syndrome
Together we make a whole	The Soulmate Syndrome
(S)he is my better half	The Incomplete Me Syndrome
It was love-at-first-sight	The Rose-Colored Glasses Syndrome
We never argue—we're perfect for each other	The Agreement Syndrome
My knight in shining armor	The Sir Lancelot Syndrome
Our love is just like the movies	The Cinema Syndrome
I will someday find a woman who is everything	The All-in-one-box Syndrome
My partner is a reflection of my value	The Trophy Syndrome
I don't have to talk because she knows me so well.	The Big Silent Type Syndrome
(S)he's a mess now, but my love will fix things	The Love-Conquers-All Syndrome

The Madison Avenue Game

Have we all been so brainwashed that we can't see clearly beyond the Madison Avenue Game?

You bet we have! How can a television show host with Dr. in their title intervene in the process of a relationship by giving global advice? Something like saying "Get real," and rewarding them for being on the show with two dozen books to read and blessing them saying "sin no more!"? We have to move beyond the unreal media images and messages to the intimacy principles and their application. (See chapter Ten). Let go of and forget the media hype—particularly script lines, behavior, which clothes to wear or what promises to make in order to entrap the other person. Can you see how ridiculous and dehumanizing that process is?

The media messages convince you that you have to earn your "wings" in a relationship by giving up a part of yourself. Not true! Such messages direct you to surrendering your own truth, values, and self respect. The currency that you use for exchanges of intimacy should be reflections of you. They are your values, your gold. It is not merely compromise that is the culprit; it is voluntary surrender of real self!

To love is to suffer. To avoid suffering one must not love. But then one suffers from not loving. Therefore to love is to suffer, not to love is to suffer.
To suffer is to suffer. To be happy is to love.
To be happy then is to suffer.
But suffering makes one unhappy.
Therefore, to be unhappy one must love,
or love to suffer, or suffer from too much happiness.
I hope you're getting this down.

—Woody Allen

Making a Commitment

So now perhaps you are ready to commit to another person. You want to "let the walls down" and have enough courage and self confidence to expose yourself (pun intended) and get really close to someone. And you want to do it without surrendering <u>you</u>!! Is it possible?

Yes! There are parts of you that don't need to shift or be compromised in the relationship process. You have ingenious elements of personality, behavior, and beliefs that can remain autonomous and vital even if they're not in concert with the other person. Respect the diversity of both of you. Accept each other the way you are and make no apologies for your truths, values, experiences.

Let me be the first to warn you that you will face the challenge of being true to yourself in the bedroom, bushes, in front of the fireplace or any other place you encounter sexual desires.

Bargaining for Intimacy

Okay, pilgrims, most likely you guessed that this topic was coming: how men and women use sex as a bargaining chip or tollgate for intimacy. Yes, sex. This is most likely the first opportunity in which someone will challenge your values and truth.

Sex. We enjoy it. We engage in it. We explore it, and unfortunately, we often use it as a currency for intimacy.

You might protest, "How could this possibly be? How could a person use such an important element of their humanness to manipulate, control or guide another person's behavior towards a predetermined outcome?"

Sit back and relax, as this subject requires some uncomfortable review and introspection. Give it a chance.

Mating Games

Consider the normal mating sequence—from the point of first communication to mutual commitment between partners. Sexuality fits into the process from the onset; perhaps not always spoken or discussed, but always lurking in the shadows. There is an unspoken knowing between male and female that engaging in sex carries with it some type of commitment, as it rightfully should.

Men need and enjoy the sexual pursuit, often taking the role of aggressor (but not always). Women also take a position on this topic as they are aware of the value of sexual surrender. They know of the man's need for the biological connection, and an obvious but insidious method of control emerges. The scenario is common, and almost comedic. The woman says, "You want to get in here and that's fine, but there's a price to pay. There are certain expectations before you even get close." Or a man might say, "I'll promise you this, this, and even that if you'll make love to me tonight."

Is this the purpose of sex and sexuality? Absolutely not!

Men and women allude to these issues typically within the third or fourth communication of the blossoming relationship. The preliminary petting ritual is typically paced and controlled by the woman, and there are more subtle messages that occur during the process of kissing and touching.

> *Consider how hard it is to change yourself and you'll understand what little chance you have of trying to change others.*
>
> —Jacob M. Brude

In the kissing and touching phases, the subtle messages could be an inquiry as to the partner's feelings. For example, a woman will back off or discourage further physical intimacy by bringing up certain issues specific to what she sees as the growth or the maturing of the relationship: *So, honey, how do you feel about me?* The translation means *Tell me that I'm special. Reinforce my position with you and my feeling that we're going to have a future together.*

These little hooks tossed out mean that the man has to respond because there is a silent agreement that this dialogue is leading to sexual intercourse. The woman might see the man's feelings as critical in obtaining that control and the commitment of the partner, knowing during this whole process what the end result will be, and milking it to the max.

On the other hand, the male dialogue might go: *You're beautiful.* Translated, that means: *I own you. You're valuable to me. With you, I am desirable.* Men have particularly strange self-created needs: to feel the woman is his alone, or that he owns her, or to feel as unique and desirable and valuable as women do, and sometimes even more. So, the idea of exclusivity, monogamy, or the need for long-term commitment is not specific only to the woman; it's multi-gendered.

For many people, exclusivity in relationships is a direct dynamic or even consequence of commitment. If you're committed, then you demand exclusivity. If you're committed to me sexually, then naturally you're monogamous.

I have no idea where this concept or idea came from. If you consider commitment in any other arena other than romance and romantic relationships, it does not reflect a need for exclusivity.

The mind is continually seeking pleasure and purpose. It is ravenous for meaning, and self-justification. It is a machine that, by itself, creates itself and then demands to be satisfied, pleasured, and, most destructively, loved.

Some "Sexist" Advice

Well, fellow travelers. Here is some advice on how to handle the issue of sexuality during the preliminary and intermediate mating ritual (after that, you're on your own!).

Never give sex value or power as an indicator or precursor of intimacy. Why? Because as soon as you do, then sex becomes a meaningless tool, and will likely be abused.

Stop the story lines running in your head. Instead, remind yourself that this could very well be the beginning of a beautiful relationship. And sex can only make it better.

Only specifically in a love or romantic relationship does there seem to be a natural expected sequence of conversation:

o   "If you want in, then I want a promise of exclusivity."
o   "If you want in, you are going to be the only one."
o   "I'm gonna be the only one, of course."
o   "What do you want me to promise for that exclusivity?"

If you meet and are attracted to someone, feel they're reasonable and safe and feel good about it, have sex and enjoy it. If you feel guilty in the morning, take two aspirin and say twelve Hail Mary's. Seriously, whether having sex on the first, second, third, or fourth date is going to affect the ultimate outcome of the relationship is your choice and perception. As soon as you start feeling that if you engage in sex too early in the relationship you are giving up a "bargaining chip," then you are controlling the relationship, and it is likely doomed to failure.

Demands for Exclusivity?

Does exclusivity always lead to being captured and capturing? Absolutely not! Fidelity and personal commitment should be CHOICES, NOT mandates. It is natural to pledge and maintain exclusivity in a relationship. However, this choice should be made not out of fear of punishment or abandonment, but out of love and loyalty.

However, for some, the reason that we demand exclusivity is a combination of our own insecurities, cultural issues, and Madison Avenue sex scripts.

This makes a choice that is pure and loving into a demand that is arduous and burdensome. There is absolutely no reason why the choice for exclusivity should not be a choice of love and mutual respect.

The seed is planted by normal accepted social behavior, but it's certainly reinforced and grows naturally in a garden of feelings such as insecurity, inadequacy, uncertainty or fear.

In other words, work towards enjoying the gift of exclusivity, rather than enduring the limitations of it. Again, sometimes easier said than done. But well worth the effect!

> *Love is the answer—but while you're waiting for the answer sex raises some pretty good questions.*
>
> —Woody Allen

The True Value and Meaning of Exclusivity

Beware! Exclusivity though generally mandatory in a loving relationship, in itself is not an indicator of intimacy, just as engaging in sex is not. Because there is continued fidelity in a relationship doesn't mean that it is healthy, beneficial, or even adequate. Yet, it doesn't mean that a truly intimate committed relationship should not be exclusive or monogamous.

Let's define terms a bit more.

Monogamy is typically viewed as sexual exclusivity (don't mess around with anyone else but me). Yet it can also be in the realm of the emotional, spiritual, and even intellectual. I've seen many couples, Keaw and myself included, seeking exclusivity in areas other than sexual.

It surprises many people that Keaw and I have a rule of exclusivity regarding prayer and meditation. Both Keaw and I feel that it is uniquely important to our relationship: one of the true experiences of intimacy that we share is spending sacred quiet time together.

Keaw would rather see me have a sexual relationship with a woman before she would concede to me meditating with another woman. Well, in my dreams, anyway.

The reason behind our agreement is that both Keaw and I share a strong love and appreciation for our individual inner journey and experience. We share our meditative awareness.

Murphy's Law in Sex

1. *No matter how many times you've had it, if it's offered take it, because it'll never be quite the same again.*
2. *Sex has no calories.*
3. *Sex takes up the least amount of time and causes the most amount of trouble.*
4. *Sex appeal is 50% what you've got and 50% what people think you've got.*
5. *Sex is like snow; you never know how many inches you are going to get or how long it is going to last.*
6. *When a man's wife begins to understand him, she usually stops listening to him.*
7. *Never sleep with anyone crazier than yourself.*
8. *The qualities that most attract a woman to a man are usually the same ones she can't stand years later.*

Exclusivity and Commitment

Exclusivity though beneficial and mutually rewarding (and safer!) is NOT necessary for commitment, or even intimacy. Now that's a mouthful!

We normally think of exclusivity in the realm of sexuality. Naturally, monogamy works best for most couples. However, exclusivity in the intellectual, emotional, or spiritual realm is NOT necessary, or even desirable.

When my wife finds a man who can engage in conversation at her intellectual level, I might very well feel threatened. It's easy for me to think that I'm deficient. I translate that thought into believing that my partner has a need that I cannot fulfill. Have you ever had similar thoughts? This merely closes doors, and creates frustration and limitation.

Yet, what if I feel it is threatening and I want to keep my wife away from people like that because my insecurity starts blossoming and gets out of control? I magnify our differences and automatically I feel that she's going to leave me. Old abandonment tapes start playing. Captured once again!

In our developing relationship, this is now mutually encouraged. She does do this, and I think it is wonderful when she has an intellectual discussion, plays a game of chess or shares abstract physics concept about which I have no clue. The experience enriches Keaw and creates no threat to our relationship.

Insecurity Stifles Intimacy

Consider the couple consisting of an overweight man and a svelte woman. The overweight man doesn't want to discuss his size, change it, or fix it, but he feels uncomfortable being overweight—especially with his shapely wife. Enter another male who is not overweight. That person immediately becomes a threat, even within a casual and perfectly innocent relationship. It is quite easy to see in this example that it is the insecurity of the man that causes the dilemma and conflict.

It is vital that each partner in a relationship understand and accept that they cannot provide all the imagined or stated needs of their partner! This is NOT a deficiency, it is merely a reality. To know this, and to allow others to enhance your partner's quality of life without feeling violated or threatened, is critical for a healthy relationship.

Variety and diversity do not create separation. Only when considered by the demanding and insecure self does this occur.

The Possibility of Multiple Lovers (Briefly)

What if you have several lovers and you're not ready to make an exclusivity commitment to only one? Would that make each relationship shallow and meaningless?

Though multiple relationships are often distractions and a reflection of the unwillingness to make a true and honest commitment, there are situations where these relationships are truly intimate, diverse and satisfying. But tread cautiously here! There are many traps inherent in these types of relationships.

> *"Did you ever have to make up your mind?*
> *Pick up on one and leave the other behind*
> *It's not often easy and not often kind*
> *Did you ever have to make up your mind?"*
> *"Did You Ever Have to Make Up Your Mind,"*
>
> © 1966, The Lovin' Spoonful

Edsel Terrick Philosophy 101: *If it reflects your nature, is not harmful to anyone (including yourself), and if it provides pleasure and joy, there's nothing wrong with it.*

Remember, sometimes even within a committed intimate relationship, sex is just sex. And that's okay. No, Dorothy, it's not all stars and stripes, colors and lights, all the time. Enjoy it when it is. Enjoy it when it isn't!

Captured and Capturing?

The huge issue of exclusivity is fertile ground for capturing someone else, or being captured. Don't surrender your values and hard-realized truths.

I hope I've made these messages clear:

o   Sexual exclusivity (monogamy) in honest relationships makes sense because it is safer and creates consistency. This works well if two committed, caring partners have chosen this based on similar beliefs.

o   Unfortunately, most of us make this choice from insecurity, living out another's love script, and then surrender our personal value. We trade ourselves as a commodity on the love exchange.

o   From that confused understanding, we group all other aspects of relationships around our sexual limitations, since sexuality is so basic to our nature and a vital part of the mating dance.

o   Such limitations and exclusivity sometimes create a tunnel that confines, suffocates and mutually imprisons us.

How to Not Satisfy Your Partner's Needs Completely

Got your attention, didn't I? It is impossible and preposterous to imagine that two people could satisfy each other's needs, demands, or expectations (realistic or otherwise) in all the different realms of human experience.

Usually, what people do in exclusive relationships is to compel, coerce, demand, manipulate and conspire to get the partner to provide what they believe that they need. This is absolutely ridiculous.

I see such silly games every day:

o   A young wife resents her husband playing basketball on Sunday afternoons when he could be with her on her only day off.

o   A middle-aged husband opposes his wife's new hobby of gardening with girlfriends on Saturday afternoons because he has chosen to stay home to be with her and never told her.

o   There is continued frustration and resentment due to the intrusion(s) of technical distractions or even involvement (see chapter on cyber-distractions).

o   A husband resents his wife taking the evening shifts as a nurse at the local hospital to offset household expenses. He likes being the only wage earner.

When I review these situations, my response is "Hello! Where did you get these expectations? Why aren't you talking to your partner? If you don't speak up, are you expecting your partner to be a mind-reader?" I hear you laughing, but most people would say, "Yes, of course, s/he knows me so well."

Does your partner really know you that well? These unrealistic expectations of intimacy are supported by those emotional "ghost" memories we discussed in previous chapters.

For women, ghost memories manifest as lack of self esteem, not knowing the value of self, or disgruntlement. For males, often all they seem to feel is anger. Hurt and disappointment are an advanced emotion for many men. A male's initial emotional reaction to most threatening events is anger. Anger is much safer, and seems to create energy to fix, alter and to change.

Violations of Intimacy

A toxic sequence of events often develops when communication becomes dishonest. Feelings of betrayal and disappointment promote behaviors that violate the very core of a relationship.

Attachment destroys courage awareness of self, and then goes on to destroy the object of attachment itself. This is a principle that on the surface appears to be a paradox, but only reflects truth. One's own experience can support this perspective, if reviewed honestly and completely.

The play often unfolds as follows:

Act I: *I don't feel emotionally connected to you.*
Act II: *You don't satisfy me sexually, intellectually, emotionally, etc.*
Act III: *I have to go somewhere else to get what I need.*
Act IV   (The Final Act):
          I'm justified in deceiving you in order to continue our relationship. At that point, even deception appears to be reasonable and acceptable. Poop!

Sound familiar? This play is acted out over and over again. The "soap operas" are full of them!

This sequence, and the ultimate delusions that come into play, will undoubtedly tear apart a relationship. Dishonesty and self-justification always diminish and eventually dissolve a relationship, even when undiscovered. Imagine that!

Getting Real and Staying Honest

No two human beings will completely satisfy each other, nor should they! This, dear reader, is a fact. In spite of what you have seen in the movies, or heard in songs, it just doesn't happen. And if it DOES appear to happen, wow, are you SUPER NO CLUE!!!

Know it. It is imperative to understand that some desires or perceived needs are met only outside of an intimate relationship. What they are, and how those needs should be satisfied is a dialogue between partners that requires honesty, open-mindedness, and mutual trust along with a strong commitment to "make it work".

This dialogue is essential. Not only in the first phases of a relationship, but in all.

Conclusion

The solutions to relationship problems and challenges can be so simple if you understand, accept and feel comfortable with yourself. Self-comfort means you are willing to grow and expose your inner life to your partner, even when such disclosures feel "wrong". You must discover your core values and true nature, express, protect and share them.

Question the creditability of stories and scripts that continue to influence your perception and reactions. Place a sentinel of awareness and reason around you so that you may fully understand that fairy tales are just that—fairy tales. Life is so much more real and so much more fun!

Refuse to live out romantic myths and unrealistic scenarios. Write your own intimacy scripts based on your identified strengths, desires, perceived needs and dreams. Never settle for a bit part, when you have the right, and responsibility, to be the star in your own show—your life!

If you don't have those skills, keep reading. I'll show you how.

Afterglow—Points to Remember

o   Emotional memories (which are tremendously strong, and sometimes hidden even from self) wrote our love stories and relationship scripts.

o   The media messages convince you that you have to earn your way by giving up a part of your innermost self. Not true.

o   Accept each other the way you are and make no apologies for your truth, values and repartee.

o   The apparent need for exclusivity and commitment is not just specific and germane to women; it's multi-gendered. The core message here is that each partner is telling the other "if there is something that you think you need that I can't provide for you, please don't go anywhere else for it." The fact is that BEFORE your partner goes elsewhere, BRING IT TO THE LIGHT! Then, if it poses no threat to you or the relationship, simply let them (as if you had a choice!). They will likely come back. And if not, forgive them.

o   The huge issue of exclusivity is fertile ground for capturing someone or being captured. Don't surrender your values and truths.

o   Unrealistic expectations of intimacy are supported by those emotional "ghost" memories.

o   No two human beings will completely satisfy each other because the mind continually generates NEW needs and demands. This is merely the nature of the mind... NOT a mistake.

o   Dialogue is essential. Question the stories and scripts that captured you and continue to affect you and keep you in tow.

o   Refuse to live out romantic myths. Instead, write your own intimacy scripts based upon your personal strengths, desires, needs and dreams.

o   Enjoy the journey, even when quite bumpy!

MALE BONDING

Chapter 4

To Love Another, Know Thyself

The importance of making an honest personal assessment of ourselves, including our nature and our own often self-created priorities in life.

> *All great truths begin as blasphemies.*
>
> —George Bernard Shaw

Looking Inside—What's There?

In the previous chapters, I've mentioned often that a true intimate relationship does not require you to surrender character traits, values, or authenticity. This fact assumes that you know yourself well enough to identify what those traits and values are. Intimacy also assumes that you are aware of your fears and insecurities so that you can be honest with your partner, share your doubts and truth, and find acceptance within your intimate's heart. If you are unsure of your deeper truths, let's start with an exploration of fear-based relationships and how we unconsciously manipulate our partner with those fears.

Fear-Based Relationships

A fear-based relationship is one defined and confined according to your, or your partner's, fears. Fear is always based on past experiences and perceptions. Once those are recorded and implanted in the mind, we go about assuming that similar events will result in something unsatisfying, uncomfortable, or downright PAINFUL!

Once we know what threatens or weakens our partners, we often use this knowledge to control or manipulate. Here is an examples of people who considered themselves open and loving, yet were limited by unconscious fears.

Eric, a forty-two year old insurance salesman stuck by his wife of fifteen years after she confessed to having an affair with a co-worker in the early years of their marriage. Why did she confess? Fear of her husband finding out and her need to unburden herself of the guilt she had carried for so long. Eric and his wife attended counseling, where good-hearted Eric confessed that he loved her dearly and that his greatest fear was his wife leaving him. Six months of rewriting their intimacy scripts through counseling seemed to work for them, and they returned to their normal life. Six more months passed, and Eric's wife started throwing barbs when she was angry at him: *I don't know why I just don't leave. You can be so heartless. Blah, blah, blah.* She takes advantage of his fear, threatening to leave him.

Here one partner is taking advantage of another's vulnerability or needs (both physical and emotional). Unknowingly and unwittingly, many people's lives and their important decisions are governed, directed, limited or controlled by fear.

> *For a male and female to live continuously together is, biologically speaking, an extremely unnatural condition.*
>
> —Robert Briffault

Fear, the Relentless Taskmaster

Fear drives us into a state of inertia and a general unwillingness to take risks. Or it seems to pressure us into exerting stifling control. Many people accept situations, lifestyles and an overall quality of life that they know is sub-standard. Truly, it is not what they deserve, want, desire or need. Yet, they would accept this rather than find the courage and willingness to face and deal with their fear. Ouchies! Captured! Yes, because of the fear that is buried deep inside, and that controls their decisions, they will not give up, or preferably, improve, an unfulfilling and shallow relationship.

I have seen friends or acquaintances stay in abusive or empty relationships. I've seen one partner physically or emotionally harm or abuse the other both by action, and inaction. The episodes seem unbelievable. How can people do that?

Look more closely to understand the fear dynamic. The fear of leaving and being without another person is so overwhelming that many decide to stay in a relationship that threatens their health, safety and very life. They actually feel safer in the pain of the victim role than understanding and being willing to experience what freedom might feel like.

Evaporation of the separateness that we have created instills even more fear and discomfort for the self. But the opportunity for true love to grow and merge and create a new oneness is thusly created. It can move no other way.

> *I do not fear failure.*
> *I only fear the "slowing up" of the engine inside of me which is*
> *pounding, saying, "Keep going, someone must be*
> *on top, why not you?"*
>
> —George S. Patton

The Pain of Nothing?

Life threatening, abusive relationships are at best mediocre and are devoid of joy. The participants' interactions in the relationships don't reflect possibility and potential. Let's face it! What people in those relationships have to look forward to is more of the same. Their vision of love is myopic, and it hurts like hell to be in such a prison with no windows and no reprieve. We might furnish and decorate the prison nicely, even with inspired landscaping, but it remains a prison.

One knows that things could and should be different and it is devastating to acknowledge that it will never be better unless we let go of something that seems utterly important. Add to that the fear of being alone, living alone and dying alone. Simply put, leaving becomes more difficult than staying because people feel threatened by the unfamiliar. Many of us reach out, exploring, imploring others for some direction, support or validity.

And, of course, we don't always get that validation because the person we're reaching out to is in the same prison. You're sharing the cell and you don't even know it.

Helloooooooooooo! Wake up; the instruction manual is in your hand!

What Happens When You Fall in Love with

A chef? (You get buttered up.)
A chauffeur? (You get taken for a ride.)
A gambler? (He cheats on you.)
A trash man? (He dumps you.)
A clockmaker? (He two-times you.)
A pastry cook? (He desserts you.)
A shoe salesman? (He walks all over you.)
An elevator operator? (He lets you down.)
An artist? (He gives you the brush.)
A jogger? (He gives you the run-around.)

Who's Your Jailer?

Have you seen pictures of elephant trainers in India standing next to their elephant whose leg is chained? The chain goes toward a post to which it was once attached. Now it is just on the ground. As an infant, the elephant was chained to the post and learned the limits of its movement. As the elephant grew older, the elephant trainer no longer needed to keep the elephant chained to the post. The elephant did not stray from the limits to which the trainer conditioned it.

Like the elephant, we become conditioned to our imprisonment. Unlike the elephant, we actually choose to be captured and continue a life full of limitation, suffocation and boredom, even after we know we have a choice. We are making that choice on a daily basis. Of course, we don't acknowledge that we are because morning, noon, night, and next morning seem to roll into each other.

It is your mind only that makes you insecure and unhappy. Anticipation makes you insecure. Memory makes you unhappy.

Time disappears when you're so habituated to the prison. We are imprisoned. And we are the jailers! Typically in such a condition of spiritual repression, an external event like my own wake-up call is effective in jarring loose the framework and rattling the bars. At least you realize that you are in prison and that the door has been wide open all along. You can walk out any time.

A good-looking person will open my eyes,
An intelligent person will open my mind,
But only a good-hearted person will open my heart.

For many people, walking out is an overwhelming threat for two reasons:

1. People are forced to look back and say, "You mean I've been staying in this jail, the door's been open all this time, and I haven't gone out? What an idiot." (That's hard to face!)
2. Even worse than realizing the door is open, is the understanding that you may not know where to go: "Where the hell am I going to go once I'm out of this prison? I have no clue. I haven't truly taken responsibility for the direction of my life. How can I do it at this point?"

Then, do you want the door closed again? The prayer would sound like: "Please Lord, take from me all possibilities and allow me to continue to be a victim so that I cannot make any mistakes—ever." I hope nobody's listening to, or SAYING, *that* prayer!

Will inspired by love, rather than Will inspired by self. Action inspired by love. Action with no objective, either inside or outside. This feels very much like emptiness. And, of course, emptiness is what many of us are continually trying to avoid. So... in a word... YIPES!

You DO Have a Choice

Yes, you do! You can choose to open the door, walk out of the prison, and take another risk for freedom and true love. Freedom is climbing onto the eagle's back, taking magical flight and rising higher to gain perspective on your life. Oh, imprisoned one, you need new vistas and endless horizons to feel inspired again. Don't settle for mediocrity despite the fearful struggle with which the mind continuously thwarts you. Change your point of view and start seeing the humor of your situation. Here's a laugh for you!

Absurd Marriage Postulates

*To be happy with a man, you must understand him a lot and love him a
    little.*
*To be happy with a woman, you must love her a lot
    and try not to understand her at all.*
*Married men live longer than single men,
    but married men are a lot more willing to go.*
*Any married man should forget his mistakes,
    there's no use in two people remembering the same thing.*
A woman marries a man expecting he will change, but he doesn't.
A man marries a woman expecting that she won't change, and she does.
A woman has the last word in any argument.
Anything a man says after that is the beginning of a new argument.
*There are two times when a man doesn't understand a woman—before
    marriage and after marriage.*

All right, we've taken a thorough look at our fears. How about a humorous view of our beliefs about relationships and marriage?

Are Relationships Naturally Homogenous?

We love images of one person merging into another. "Two become one." How idyllic! How preposterous! Why would you want to be devoured so completely, unless you were a lonely lamb chop?

Constant differences and fluidity make relationships real. One person feels good and one person feels lousy. There comes an evening where one partner feels amorous and loving, and the other partner feels like "Is it you again?" or "I'm bored, I don't feel now like I did yesterday about you."

"What have we lost? What has changed?"

Sound familiar?

Accepting the Unacceptable

Somewhere along the line you've said or thought: "You know the good feelings are gone. I can't expect them, and maybe I don't even deserve them. I'll just stay with the bad feelings and that's okay."

You compromise and say "I'll just stay where I am because I don't want to change it because I'm afraid." Captured again, baby, every time you want an escape route! And it isn't real; it's just in your head.

> *The perfect lover is one who turns into a pizza at 4:00 A.M*
>
> —Charles P. Pierce

The Case of Joe and Judy

Joe falls madly in love with Judy. They move in together and spend exciting and passionate hours exploring each others' lives, psyches and bodies. They are on their best behavior for the first year, and it seems to be smooth sailing.

Then, Joe complains to whoever will listen that Judy has changed. She works longer hours, doesn't share conversations like she used to, doesn't seem interested any more.

You know the story, right? You've probably lived it yourself. The real question is, "Joe, has your partner changed?"

Who Is Changing?

Let's reexamine the assumption that Joe's partner is changing. I would suspect that Judy is becoming more real,,, finally, being more of who she always was. Early in a relationship or love affair, you're on your best behavior. Time passes, and you're more comfortable with each other. It is often at this point that reality bites: Your partner is who they always were, but probably *more* so! The sugar-coating is gone. The pink cloud has matured into cold rain.

Two Truths:

o   You're probably just seeing them differently, and more than likely your expectations were unrealistic from the very beginning. You saw who you wanted to see, rather than who WAS.

o   You are bringing into the relationship your own changes of perception and/or your own honest discovery or modification of your own needs that you haven't acknowledged before.

From Philosophy to Reality

From a man's perspective, I can say categorically that if I'm in need of sex (horny), just about any woman is looking good! And, once satisfied, my very perception is altered. I suddenly see all kind of flaws, inadequacies and annoyances since my need is satisfied! Come on guys.... CONFESS!

Women actually smell and feel different after sex. Don't believe me? Ask your man!

Is It Love?

Bill and Steve are discussing the possibility of love.
"I thought I was in love three times," Bill says.
"Thought?" Steve asks. "What do you mean?"
"Three years ago, I cared very deeply for a woman who wanted
*   nothing to do with me,"*
Bill says. "Wasn't that love?" Steve asks.
"No, that was obsession," Bill explains. "Then two years ago, I cared
*   very deeply for an attractive woman who didn't understand me."*
"Wasn't that love?" asks Steve.
"No, that was lust," Bill replies. "And just last year, I met a woman
*   while I was on a cruise. She was gorgeous, intelligent, a great*
*   conversationalist and had a super sense of humor.*
Everywhere I followed her on that ship, I would get a very
*   strange sensation in the pit of my stomach."*
"Well, wasn't that love," asks Steve.
"No. That was motion sickness!" Bill replies.

Your Partner Doesn't Change

Point: Chances are, your partner isn't changing, but the way you feel about him or her changes. So Joe, when you wake up in the morning and feel that your girl has changed, you might be pointing the finger at the wrong person. More than likely, you've changed and are seeing things differently.

In his book, *Creating a Spiritual Relationship*, Paul Ferrini explains that relationship is the most challenging spiritual path available to us for several reasons. One reason is that relationships bring our insecurities and fears to the forefront. We must be courageous to actually SEE and understand those parts of ourselves mirrored back to us. And all of this without judgment or self-condemnation.

Yet we can make peace with ourselves by making peace with our partners. This is wholeness, and we can achieve it because we feel safe with our partner.

"Relationship is not just a quest for the romantic myth of happiness. That quest is over and done with in the first year for most couples.
It is much more challenging than that. It is a quest for the Holy Grail itself, for authenticity in the midst of compromise,
for understanding in the midst of pain.
It is a shamanic journey with all of its unexpected twists and turns along the way. Sometimes it seems that our partner is more our adversary or opponent than our companion and friend.
The face we see in the mirror is always changing."

—Paul Ferrini

Knowing the Problem is the Beginning of the Solution

Well, fellow traveler, now that you've realized that pointing fingers at others (even your dearest one) is not part of the solution, you are finally on a path of true honesty and intimacy in all of your relationships.

Chapter Six will bring you wonderfully closer!

Afterglow—Points to Remember

- Intimacy assumes that you are aware of your fears and insecurities so that you can be honest with your partner, share your doubts and truth and find acceptance within your intimate's heart.
- Unknowingly and unwittingly, many people's lives and their important decisions are governed, directed, limited, or controlled by fear.

- Life-threatening, abusive relationships are mediocre and contain no joy. Typically in a condition of spiritual repression, an external event like my own wakeup call is effective in jarring the framework and rattling the bars.
- Freedom is climbing onto the eagle's back, taking magical flight and rising higher to gain perspective on your life
- Constant differences and fluidity make relationships real.
- Partners aren't changing. What changes is how you feel and perceive them.
- Relationships bring our insecurities and fears to the forefront. We must be courageous to see those parts of ourselves mirrored back to us, accurately and honestly.

I need a woman who wears WA WA perfume!
I need a man who drives a Borche!
If I wear YAXE cologne...women will love me!
If I buy BOGO JEANS my butt will look just like that!

Chapter 5

Technology's Effect on Intimacy, Self, and Relationships

It is disquieting and intensely important to understand how our "technocracy" has altered the very essence and experience of self, and thusly LIFE!

As if Life and Relationships with ourselves and others aren't enough... along comes the INTERNET!!!!

A healthy, and life-promoting relationship is always based on knowing oneself as we are, and allowing others, and the world, to be as they are. Unfortunately, the advent of the use of the internet to "connect" has been a tremendous threat to that process.

From the time we are babies, we develop what psychologists term "self-identities". This is merely the way the mind sees, and what specific elements of self creates the "me", and defines itself, the relationship of the world to this established "self",

It takes a great deal of sensitivity to understand and realize that the way we see ourselves is the way we see others. The natural tendency to feel disconnected to others, and to be uniquely discreet, is a very difficult tendency to avoid.

As a source of information and assimilation, we look outward to the world in which we live for feedback that also shapes our self-identities. Because we are fundamentally social beings and an essential part of our development involves finding our place in the social and cultural context in which we live, feedback from that social world plays a significant role in the evolution of our self-identities.

A Bigger Issue than we Realize...

Typically, the complaint that partners have about cell phones and the pervasive nature if the internet is that it distracts attention from them, and they feel ignored and abandoned. Though this is certainly justified, there is much more going on in this sea of massive information exchange!

Because the information about the world that we receive, and the communication opportunities and patterns that have expanded dramatically in the last decade, it isn't difficult to see how external forces are gaining a disproportionate influence over our self-identities compared to previous generations. And these social influences, accelerated by the recent explosion of technology, may be shaping our self-identities in ways in which most of us aren't the least bit aware. And understanding that we often view the world and others as we view ourselves, wow, are we in a heap of trouble!!!

This pervasive technology is altering self-identity from being internally to externally driven. Social factors have always had an impact on the formation of self-identity, but they had been, up until recently, partners of sorts with our own internal contributors to self-identity. But now the sheer ubiquity and force of the latest technological advances has taken that influence and turned its volume up to a deafening roar.

In previous generations, most of the social forces that influenced our self-identities were positive and predictable; parents, peers, schools, communities, extracurricular activities, even the media sent mostly healthy messages about who we were and how we should perceive ourselves and treat others.

Of course, there were always some bad influences, but they were far outweighed by those that were beneficial, and more importantly, reality based! These various forces acted mostly as a mirror reflecting back on us what we saw in ourselves, resulting in affirmation rather than change in our self-identities.

But now, the pendulum has swung to the other extreme in a social world where the profit motive rules and healthy influences are mostly drowned out by the cacophony of the latest technology. The self-identities of this generation of young people and, in fact, anyone who is deeply immersed in popular culture and media, are now shaped by external forces in two ways.

First, popular culture no longer holds a mirror to reflect accurate self-identities. Nor does it provide feedback about how grounded our self-identities are in the reality of our lives.

Instead, popular culture manufactures "portraits" of who it wants us to be. Tapping into our most basic needs to feel good about themselves, accepted, and attractive, popular culture tells us what we should believe about ourselves, and, unfortunately, what we should expect and DEMAND from others we are in a relationship with.

Busy Energy versus Creative Energy

With electronic devices, the emphasis is on "busy" and complete absorption. The activity is motivated by the desire for strong distractions, curiosity, the inherent need to connect, and to be recognized and acknowledged and, (hopefully) accepted.

But these are all smoke and mirrors! The entirety of the communication consists of images and sounds. Some real, some not. Of course, our minds assume reality, when there is none.

In fact and practice, this way of (not) communicating has an insidious element of blocking and actually denying real individuality and uniqueness. Our very creativity is denied.

Relationships themselves are a product and function of our innate creative nature. This is truly part of our very humanness. Without realizing it, we often become part of the machine(s) we are using, rather than treating them merely as the tool that they are. And, unfortunately, they don't even appreciate it!!!!

The Origin of the Dream...

Self-identity and perceived needs that are shaped and controlled by popular culture, especially through convenient but artificial messages that serve their own best interests rather than what is best for us, are in fact toxic and spiritually debilitating.

Our very reality is derived from "stories" and "scripts" designed to either entertain, distract, or more ominously, comply and "belong"

> *I said to my mate, "You should treat your girlfriend the same way you treat your cell phone."*
> *He said, "What, take good care of her, and never lose her."*
> *I said, "No, upgrade every couple of years."*

The goal for many now in their use of social media becomes how they can create acceptance, popularity, status, and, by extension, a positive image of self, whatever that might be! Self-awareness, honesty, and genuine self-expression give way to "image creation and management, and self-promotion based on artificially derived and promoted standards.

We come to see our own identities, and even the identities of those we are committed to, as what we want people to discern, rather than what they really are.

The thin line between real and fantasy, truth and lies, genuine and contrived, become blurred or erased completely and the so-called self-identity and the very nature and dynamics of our relationships become a means of our ceaseless need for acceptance, approval, satisfaction and status.

In the "cyber world" we unwittingly sacrifice our true self-identities and shape our identities to conform to what the digital world views as acceptable identity. And, in doing so, we relinquish the specialness that is so truly valuable, not only of ourselves, but even of our loved ones!

There are two really sad things about this unintended consequence of the use of these emerging technologies. First, most people have no idea of the dramatic changes that are occurring slowly yet inexorably within them and their precious but delicate relationships.

Second, this shift in identity, from internally derived to externally driven, can't be good for us as individuals nor ultimately supportive and nurturing in our relationships.

Compliment her!
Take her someplace nice!
Wait three days to call!
Be COOL!
Chicks like an aggressive man!
Be Nice!
Pay for everything!
JUST DO HER
Avoid her!
Be Sensitive!
Women LOVE bad boys
Just whip it out!
Don't bring flowers!
Call her immediately!
Talk about your pets!
Ask about her day!
Ignore her!
Make her pay half!
Don't be sensitive!
Listen to Her!
Meet her parents!
Don't rush into a physical relationship!
10 EASY STEPS TO SUCCESSFUL DATING!
How 2 B a PLAYA
Meet available ladies in your town tonight!
HOW TO MEET WOMEN
LONELY?
Call GALS
WwwMateMatch
Order from the menu for her!
Get her in the sack as soon as possible!
Bring her flowers!

The Value of Honesty and Openness in Relationships

How to share your personal nature and truths with your lover, and become closer and closer . . . .

Defining Purpose

A primary committed relationship is a beautiful and tremendously important part of your life. Now it's time to ask why. Author Paul Ferrini's point that relationships can be the most valuable spiritual path on the planet today, as well as our discussions of intimacy thus far, bring us to that very question: What is the purpose of a committed relationship?

There are as many answers to this question as there are people asking it. Since we're on a journey of self-discovery and awareness, let's see what your answer is.

Choose the answer(s) that best reflects your perspective and personality.

I believe that the main purpose of my primary relationship is:

o   To have company and/or companionship,
o   To be taken care of in times of need (and when cold, hungry or horny),
o   To be supported (financially, emotionally, or sometimes even physically),
o   To be nurtured and/or understood by another,

o   To be defended or protected,
o   To *not* feel lonely, or alone,
o   To have someone with whom to share interests and activities,
o   To share living expenses and household chores with,
o   To feel loved,
o   To have someone to talk to besides my dog or cat,
o   To have someone to grow old with, and/or
o   To placate society, parents (or dog) who want you to want it.

Ask the Right Questions and Find the Right Answers. Or Just STOP Asking Questions!

How you answered these questions is vitally important because they determine what your needs, expectations and ultimately DEMANDS are from your chosen partner. Based upon your needs, now list your objectives for <u>your</u> intimate relationship.

My Objectives in Relationship Are:

1.
2.
3.
4.
5.
6.

Are they reasonable? Are they obtainable? Note the most important ones, or, better yet, rank their order of importance to you.

Needless to say, (but I'll say it anyway), honesty is imperative here, just as it is in the whole process that you have commenced. Remember, there really *are* no wrong answers.

Now that you have pinpointed what your relationship expectations are, let's consider what parameters you are using to determine success.

A Walk Down Memory Lane

How often do you revisit images and feelings from past relationships with a feeling of disappointment and sadness? Or possibly with exuberance and the very thrill of courting? Ahhhhh... the magic of the first kiss and sexy and mysterious first touches? Discovering the other person and presenting yourself, and receiving acceptance? Remember the feelings of nurturing and valuing and accepting that went with that? Wow, that was a great time. What happened?

First, it's vitally important to understand that the mind DOES NOT store experience in different "boxes" or files. This is especially true of emotional memories. Things and events are perceived, analyzed, discerned, related to other experiences already in memory, AND projected to the imagined "future" with regard to how this information might effect future outcomes... ALL based on desire for pleasure and comfort.

Can you see how even watching a movie, reading a book, listening to a story, or experiencing an event becomes another element in your "memory pool". Always prepared to be re-focused upon and compared to what is happening or what might be projected to happen.

OK, this is quite a leap for most minds. But they don't call me Edsel Terrick for nothing!!!!

Second, it's important to understand the nature and dynamic specifically of what I call "emotional memories".

The events that were the basis or foundation of such memories are often forgotten. The actual event(s) are at best distorted or obscured. But the mind desires to recreate these pleasant feelings, one way or another! It just forgets how (or, more likely, never knew how to begin with!)

You know (or strongly believe) that:

- The relationship has changed.
- You can't go back in time and begin again (though some have tried).
- You've changed (yes, we do that every day, and every moment).
- Starting the same process with another person just to re-capture those early feelings and experiences leaves you without integrity,

trust and loyalty—certainly no foundation for the quality of life that you are seeking, nor a satisfactory basis for the new relationship.

It is necessary that you acknowledge that there was strong sense of elation and joy in the beginning. The flame of passion burned brightly. You were not crazy or stupid for making the choices that you did. Well, then again, maybe you were... but that's often just what we are!

Rebirthing the Baby

Many of us know the feelings and experiences of being a new parent of an innocent, naturally loving and dependent infant. There is wonderful joy in the tremendous physical, emotional and spiritual fulfillment for the parents, especially the mom who might be breastfeeding or is certainly the primary source of nurturing and survival for the child.

Then, the infant starts growing—baby—toddler—child.

Is there any loss here? It often feels like it, but in fact there is none. Only change. Of course it was special at the beginning, and it will *never* be the same. But, darlings, it's not supposed to be! The human experience consists of change and transition by its very nature.

"So," you ask patiently, "What does this possibly have to do with the fact that the thrill seems to be gone in my intimate relation?"

Don't attempt to be newlyweds again and make believe things haven't changed. They have! Rather, if you must, conjure up or revisit those emotional memories of the "good old times".

But here's the big challenge... Make them present in your life NOW. Do you know when you first fell in love? Do you remember when you had your first date? Can you recall those heart-felt feelings? Answering these questions is a reminder of the good feelings you have the ability to recall. Doing this is NOT a solution to the problem that you have so effectively created! It is only the first step to dealing with any feelings of loss in your present relationship. But now the biggest and ultimately most rewarding challenge—to create new and better ones!

And the Next Step Is . . .

One point of difficulty for relationships, as well as for me to deal with in my relationship with Keaw, is this: What do I do when my partner no longer seems to be my ally or cheerleader (of course based on my inaccurate but REAL perspective)?

Now we can substitute any word you wish for cheerleader: support, best friend, confidante, unconditional lover, life partner forever and so on. When your partner no longer in seems to be playing that role in which you valued and cherished them, and/or when their role changes, what do you do? (Besides feeling betrayed!).

Often, my day goes like this: I'm feeling like I'm in an arena fighting wild animals, and I'm constantly being attacked and challenged by people and their problems. I feel swordsman-like, strong, and powerful. I hold up my sword, but the sword grows heavier. I'm still swinging it and trying to get through the day. Small hurts and disappointments, and then major calamities come up. Business distresses and emotional extremes characterize my day.

"More drama," you say? Hey, I can handle it.

While driving, I sag in my seat, and when I arrive home, I slither out of the car. I meander up the stairs, hope the door is unlocked, but it is not. My irritation escalates as I imagine that the locked door is a secret message from my beloved who stands behind the door with a laser-zap gun.

Too much? Okay I don't want to be unreasonable.

Yes, I can find my key, unlock the door, and walk in to find that my partner is caring for the children. But I'm an adult, so I give her some latitude, and I understand that the children need to be taken care of, but so do I.

I make a quick reality shift. Before I can get a word out, my wife bombards me with all the kids' problems. She hands me the mail with 17 bills due. Now psychically, intellectually and emotionally, the world (and my hitherto beloved partner) is the enemy, and I remember that before I had a safe refuge with my partner and ally on my side. Treason!!!

Yet, at this particular moment, I feel like I've been totally abandoned.

Have you had a variation of this experience?

For many, this is not a time to share hurt feelings. Too risky! Rather this is a time for survival and psychic and emotional protection, the perfect ingredients for a battle.

At that moment, what do you do?

What-to-Do Quiz

1. Do you demand that your partner pay attention to you?
2. Do you throw a fit in front of your children?
3. Do you sigh loudly enough for her to hear and wait for attention?
4. Do you huff away, pouting until he or she gets the hint and runs after you?
5. Do you request nicely that your partner drop all their other concerns and responsibilities and take care of your needs?
6. Do you go to the fridge, grab a beer and plop in front of the television?
7. Do you drop everything to run and help your partner?
8. Do you quietly sneak in, peck your partner on the cheek, tip-toe to the bedroom to change clothes and pray she doesn't ask for your help?
9. Do you speak your complaints more loudly than his or hers, hoping to win a contest?

    Do you shrug your shoulders and go about your evening?
10. Do you start texting on your cell phone, or more harmfully start engaging in "cyber relationships" on the internet (see Chapter 5!).

As in any other situations that we experience, before you come to a solution, you have to acknowledge the problem, and, even more importantly, what (or more likely WHO, is the source of the problem!). If we all were two years old, we could kick our feet, have a temper tantrum, and maybe get our way.

However, there is a better way.

> *Let me be your freedom,*
> *let daylight dry your tears.*
> *I'm here with you, beside you,*
> *to guard you and to guide you . . .*
>
> "All I Ask of You" by Andrew Lloyd Webber and Charles Hart

The solution is realizing that there will always be times when you need an advocate other than your intimate, and you might find that ally outside your intimate relationship.

That advocate could be friend, a family member, a priest or rabbi. All of us need to retreat and get perspective, and still feel some support, love and understanding, even when it's not available from the person whom we expect to provide it. Of course, we know the result if we try to get support from someone who is either not able or not willing to give it at this particular time.

Getting Fed

There's an old expression that says, "don't go to a bull when you are in need of milk". And if you go to the bull when you need milk, prepare to be kicked and not fed. And remember it is NOT the fault of the proverbial bull!

This principle is totally applicable in a committed, monogamous, intimate relationship. If your need for protection, satisfaction and fulfillment are totally dependent on another person, and that other person is not available to meet those needs, it is <u>your</u> responsibility to find an alternative, in advance. In other words, it is your responsibility to meet your needs and not rely upon another who may be unavailable because of other obligations and responsibilities.

Know that there is no pairing, no coupling that guarantees each person is able to fulfill and support the other's needs a hundred percent of the time.

If you accept that your need is a very strong one, feeling to you at that moment to be the same as you need to breathe or to eat, then you must pay attention to it. The adult says, "I have a created and now apparently real need that cannot be met by my intimate partner, I am grown up enough to know that this is not really a violation, this is not a betrayal, even though it feels like it is."

> *It is better to light a single candle*
> *than to curse the darkness.*
>
> —Chinese proverb

Where else can you go to get this perceived need met, even partially, so you don't have resentment, anger or any ill feelings towards the person who can't meet these needs? We have to give permission to ourselves and our partners to find friendships, companions or emotional intimacy outside of marriage that doesn't violate our fidelity and moral standards.

Letting Others In

True intimacy is supported by allowing other intimate relationships to support the primary intimate relationship. This concept is confusing for many. Most people define the pure, wonderful intimate relationship that we discussed in the beginning of the book, as "you and me, me and you, together forever, and we need nobody else." It feels cozy, but rarely works. If you go along those lines, sooner or later, your relationship will fail. With either a dull thud, or a loud BOOM!

> *I got you babe.*
> *I got you babe.*
> *I got you babe.*
> *I got you babe.*
>
> Sonny and Cher

Betrayed!

Then to further complicate and exacerbate the situation we believe that we've betrayed our partner because we've gone somewhere else to get our psychic or emotional needs met. You could twist it around and say, "I expected you to be my everything, and you're not. I had to go somewhere else, so I'm going to stick my tongue out and hate you." There's that two-year-old again.

In mature relationships, intimacy is <u>not</u> all or nothing.

Chief Cook and Bottle Washer

It's not only in the emotional and spiritual realm that many of us make errors regarding what should be expected or demanded from our primary partner. It is amazing to me (yes, I've done it too) how easily we slip into the belief that our mate should be good at everything, especially the things that are important to us.

Case in point: My wife is totally lousy at mechanics and house maintenance (such a GIRL!), and is not a tremendously good writer (English is her second language... so you see the foolishness of my expectations! But do I?. So, what to do? What to do?

Does it makes sense that I exert influence or pressure in some way to improve her mechanical skills? Maybe send her to carpentry or wood-working school. Or have her trained by a professional builder to teach her to be what I want her to be, and to know, and to like. Or maybe keep complaining and nagging until she feels *so* bad that she miraculously learns to do what she can't do. Duhhhh!

Or, there's a better idea. I have applied it. Maybe you should too . . .

Prioritize!

Keaw is a wonderful wife and mother. She is loving, affectionate, loyal, sexy, sensual, playful, honest, spirited, and has a great smile (though she has been known to do the "Thailand Stomp"—contact me and I'll tell you what that is!). She's a fantastic cook and house-keeper And even pitches in (better than I quite often) to bring money into the family. She is devoted, nurturing, sensitive, understanding, patient and playful.

So, I complain about her not being a good builder? WHAT!!!???That is *not* her role, it's not at the center (or anywhere near) of our relationship.

It's imperative for me that I acknowledge her value, and put what I judge to be her "deficiencies" in perspective. If I need a mechanic or carpenter, I can hire one or let the things just be the way they are. If we want professional services, we can seek and hire a professional.

I didn't marry her to do this! My demands are unreasonable and unobtainable. So I need to surrender, understand, accept and love her for the wonderful woman that she is. So, far, one day at a time, I've done this. And she has done the same for me.

The Meaning of Life

Someone said that life is a learning experience. Once, after an AA meeting, I stopped the woman who made the presentation and said, "I really enjoy what you said about life being a learning experience. What I can't figure out is what the final exam is and what is the reward for learning? Or even what is the value of this imagined learning!

"Well, I haven't quite figured that one out, but in practice, on a day-to-day basis, it's good for me to think this way." she replied.

That sounded satisfactory to me, so I'd like to develop this concept further and look at life as a learning laboratory opportunity. The objective is to learn things, realize that the learning experiences are merely experiences and be sensitive to discover and apply truths and principles from INSIDE, before you die. In other words, the objective is not to die wise and knowledgeable, but to *be* wise and knowledgeable before you die so as to derive some benefit from your awareness of your real self.

If you see being in intimate relationships is a learning experience, then stop learning! Work solely at evolving quickly as a person. Develop genuine instinct about how relationships can be successful based on self-awareness. Don't wait until you're too old to enjoy it thoroughly, if ever. We already know that youth is wasted on the young.

Every day is precious. True, intimate relationships, and even casual relationships, enhance your experience as a human being. Now is the time to make them better. In spite of whatever mistakes you've made, you can change what doesn't work and have wonderful relationships now if you understand and apply these principles.

In Summary

Don't come up with excuses, saying, "I've been hurt before. I don't want to be hurt again." "It's too much work, or obviously, I'm socially deficient." Or, "my partner is a loser, so why should I even bother, so just forget about relationships, I'll just live the rest of my life lonely and disconnected."

That's ridiculous. Why? Because relationships that are true, honest, genuine and sincere always enhance. They never detract. And always promote growth and joy.

Afterglow—Points to Remember

- Know your purpose in your committed relationship.
- Conjuring up the "ghostly" great-feeling memories of first falling in love is natural, and inevitable. This merely helps you become aware of feelings of apparent loss in your present relationship. But you need to go further.
- When your partner is no longer in the role you cherished or even projected, or when the role changes, realize that you might need another friend other than your intimate. Or, re-examine the validity and reality of what you consider "needs".
- True intimacy is supported by allowing other intimate relationships to support the primary intimate relationship.
- In mature relationships, intimacy is not all or nothing.
- If being in intimate relationships is a learning experience for you, then work at evolving quickly as a person. Stop learning, and start BEING! Develop genuine skills to make your relationships successful and be sensitive to changes as they occur.

Can't You feel the rush of freedom!!!???
INCONSISTENCIES
DISAPPOINTMENTS
UNREASONABLE EXPECTATIONS
BETRAYALS
DEMANDS
UNRESOLVED ISSUES
RESENTMENTS

Chapter 7

Out with the Old... In with the New

*Giving up the behaviors and false ideas that limit
our closeness and intimacy.*

False Ideas and Unrealistic Pictures

In earlier chapters, we've discussed (ad nauseum due to the importance of the topic!) how you probably run and believe unrealistic pictures of love... because you are caught in the web of romantic media myths and social media conspiracies. Our relationship scripts are mostly a matter of finding someone to co-star in our personal production, and remembering and re-experiencing how good it feels (or felt). What!? Second-hand feelings? Exactly!

In this chapter, we'll examine the scripts that make sense for us and those that don't, and then sort them out. I will ask you to acknowledge, and possibly give up some of the romantic pictures in your head that don't work for you and probably weren't true from the very beginning. Are you willing to let it go and try something new?

> *Love and concern for all are not things some of us are born with and others are not. Rather, they are results of what we do with our minds: We can choose to transform our minds so that they embody love, or we can allow them to develop habits and false concepts of separation.*
>
> —Sharon Salzberg, *The Force of Kindness*

Here's a test for your willingness to let go of old pictures and open new doors for true intimacy.

Quiz: What Is Your Picture of Sexy, Sensual and Stimulating?

Here are some choices—or come up with your own:

1. Scarlett O'Hara's dark ringlets, ivory complexion and peek-a-boo boobs?
2. Flat abs, muscular torso and tapering waist?
3. The hot mover like Britney with the long blonde swirls and curves?
4. The Zorro Latin machismo of broad-shoulders, dark eyes, and handsome mustached face?
5. The rounded fullness of hips, breasts, lips and eyes like Beyoncé?
6. Brad's blonde look: blue intense eyes, dashing smile and smell of prowess?
7. The dashing dare-devil pirate like a lustful Johnny to whisk you away?
8. Angelina's dancing eyes, deep wisdom, imaginal fancy and curvaceous body?
9. The sweaty locks and dreamy lyrics of Lenny?
10. The broad-shouldered strength, discipline and work hard/play hard ethics of Kobe?

Obviously, this quiz has no definitive right or wrong answers. However, it is vital at this point in your journey that you realize that certain visual images and stories provoke and stimulate exciting reactions in the mind (mostly derived from the nemesis, "Emotional Memories", and subsequent passionate feelings (more about passion in a few minutes).

So here's an important question. Do our fantasies and stories have anything (or everything) to do with our intimate relationships in real life?

I believe it is exactly this connection that we need to explore, share and sometimes see and change.

The Dilemma and Paradox of Fantasy vs. Reality

It is the seeking of the "Special One" that creates frustration and distress. There is no perfect mate, no "other half". We are complete in ourselves, and the mere insistence of believing and acting otherwise is the origin of much sorrow and discouragement. Nothing and nobody makes the perfect more perfect, for such a movement is impossible. It's like trying to add numbers to what is already infinite. It cannot be done. And the attempt creates frustration and disillusionment... And even anger.

The images that we have formulated, and their subsequent use as a schematic, benchmark or foundation for our real-life relationships keep us miserably frustrated, morbidly disappointed, and undeniably imprisoned. This is a powerful statement; yet an even larger truth looms ahead.

How many people keep searching for the right, idealized, perfect version of their mate? Read the "soul-mate wanted" columns! People have a very definite pre-conceived image and composite of not only the physical attributes of their future mate, but the mental, emotional, and spiritual attributes as well. How preposterous this is! Why not enjoy the process of discovery?

Living the Dream?

Here's a story that makes the point:

"I must have read a book about Vikings in my youth. Unknowingly, the images were indelibly etched in my mind. I constructed and stored this image of the perfect physical specimen for my mate, straight out of the Viking novel: six feet tall; broad, strong shoulders; a head full of thick, wavy hair that hung to his shoulders; full facial beard, trimmed; and hard, muscular legs. Along with this image, I imagined how life would be once I captured this partner. Idyllic for sure. Feelings of contentment and completeness worth working for!

"But alas, I've been married three times. Two of the men I married had an average build (some spare tire), were about 5' 10", and had not enough hair on the head, and much too much hair on other parts of their bodies! Of course, when things didn't quite "work out" with these men, I attributed it to their physical shortcomings. I desperately needed to meet my ideal mate.

"Then finally it happened. I met the man of my dreams. I knew that if I could just have this man, my life would look and feel the way I wanted and needed it to."

For those readers who have been "around the block" a few times like many of us have, you already know the ending of this story.

Our heroine married her hero. And, as is most often the case, the marriage ended disastrously! And the poor woman ended up with the feeling that it was hopeless, useless and futile. A truly intimate relationship would always be unobtainable for her. Sound familiar?

> *We all have a childhood dream that when there is love,*
> *everything goes like silk, but the reality is that*
> *marriage requires a lot of compromise.*
>
> —Raquel Welch

Let's discuss next how images in our head may or may not serve your goal of true, intimate relationships.

Always Rise to the Challenge

Throughout this book we're challenging the roles that make us captured and drive us to capture others. The fact is that those dynamics are happening all the time. We're not going to eliminate them. What we are learning to do is acknowledge them, define them, limit them, and even play with them.

The Soulmate Trap

Surely you've heard the phrases: *"Meet my Soulmate. May I introduce my other half? Please meet my better half."* Really? Are you kidding me???? Do you realize that you are saying that you are incomplete as human being? This is at best inaccurate, and at worst, self-demeaning. This is the one I really love: *"Meet my twin flame."* My response is "Huh?"

As a human being you are as incomplete, or complete, as I am. We were born that way. and we will die that way. Along the way we find distractions in order *not* to experience feeling incomplete: work, career, power, wealth, prestige, projects, education, politics, wars, the internet, cell phones, and CNN. Any of these items keep us busy while distracting us. Of course, when used properly these activities and experiences can be healthy and promote joy and feelings of achievement and life.

Yet all of us who have gone through that know that at the end of those roads is still a feeling of incompleteness. We all *know* that.

People need a hook to hang their picture on. That hook is often our partner. When the picture appears crooked, or faded, or generally incorrect, it's very easy to blame the hook, and seek another. Then a new picture is created, and the new partner is merely another hook.

Follow the Leader?

I can easily recall a movie scene in which two people are so intermeshed and have such a good fit, that the two literally become one. In this epitome of love and enmeshment, they are no longer individuals. Now it's just some ooze of completeness. "Let's melt together, sweetheart."

However, those of us who have traveled that road have learned a lesson. Even though for a sequence of moments, we lose ourselves, and in losing ourselves feel completeness, the feeling is temporary. Sooner than later, that particular music dies and ultimately stops. The silence that follows becomes deafening!

Ah! How do we react? You know the chorus by now: *"Obviously I've chosen the wrong mate. They've changed. Even worse, it was a good choice, they haven't changed, but I have changed. I have grown. I met this person this morning. We clicked right away. We knew that we were destined to meet. I had wonderful, absolutely joyous sex with this person for three hours. Had lunch and we discovered that we even shared the same food preferences. I knew I had found my cosmic match. However, by mid-afternoon I got an uneasy feeling in my gut. I had to acknowledge and honor that. Time to dump this loser!*

When the Music Stops

Yes, to some degree, we all act out this complete yet incomplete script. Sometimes it takes a day, sometimes a week or a month, maybe fifty years. But the story line is the same. We know that what we were feeling before is not what we're feeling now. The "bad" feelings and personal realities that seemed to be relieved before are not being relieved now. And we insist that there's a problem! We just can't figure out who created it, and even more importantly how to fix it.

Is the fallacy of the cosmic match a valid basis for a successful relationship?

You passed that quiz! No. It's not.

Rather it is a wonderful, exciting, spirited way to begin. Then we hit reality. And it's even better!

Are Republicans Worth Loving?

I was amused recently by a particular ruse to determine match parameters between dates when I was clicking through an online dating site. The web site identifies and disseminates elements of one's personality and preferences for your perfect match. One person looking for their cosmic match stated emphatically in their ad: "Republicans need not reply." Another one stated brazenly that if you "voted for Bush, don't bother me." "Ouch" said the elephant!

Besides being ludicrously funny, these people looking for a match were severely out of alignment with reality. You would think that this was a parody, but it's not. People are truly feeling that they can find their perfect partner by disseminating and discriminating these different elements like republicanism and voting preferences. This also begs the question, "What does your internal match-making system discern as the worthy elements in your partner?"

People truly delude themselves into believing that if they approach relationships in this manner, by going through the online dating process, that they can avoid mistakes in choosing the perfect partner. Once that partner is chosen, they believe that the relationship will develop positively and result in "'til death do us part."

How ridiculous this is. Even Republicans need love. And if you believe that political affiliation is the basis for your good relationship, please read on and consider changing your mind.

The Wonderful (and Unpredictable) Dance of Intimacy

The real dance of intimacy is the music called change and diversity. Tempos differ and rhythms shift. Do you remember what it feels like to get out on the dance floor? You let the beat carry you. You pose your body, smile, maybe even close your eyes to tune into your body and your partner's body. Then you move in the rhythm of the music. Every move is unexpected, and exciting.

A partnership is like being on the dance floor. Okay—it *is* inevitable that you will get your feet stepped on periodically. Or your perfect partner will inadvertently pass gas! We're not always doing the same steps or even hearing the same music!

How do you choose your rhythm, and decide on what steps you do?

Imagine how you want to see yourself in your relationship. I suggest you be loose and open, relaxed and kind. You have a set rhythm in your day that moves you through events and tasks. Is your partner an event that is scheduled in your day, like lunch and exercise? Similarly, your intimate relationship has a progressive pulse that changes rhythms each day. Each day is a new dance, allowing you to avoid hanging on to yesterday or having behavioral expectations for tomorrow.

o   Be here, now and present with your partner.
o   Be real and authentic with your partner.
o   Visualize yourself being open and tuning in to yourself as well your intimate.

You are able to achieve this with your partner after having been on the dance floor through many twirls and dips. Intimacy comes not only from your attitude and willingness, but also from your experiences and subsequent acceptance.

In the middle of harvesting, one of the farmhands had to obey the
*   call of nature.*
He went to the edge of the field and started to pee. Most
*   unfortunately, he was stung by a bee right on the tip of his penis.*
The pain was unbearable, but he remembered a piece of good advice.
He went to the farmer's house and put his penis in buttermilk.
At that moment, the farmer's daughter walked in.
Her face red, she stood perfectly still looking at him.
"Have you never seen one of these before?" the farmhand asked.
To which the girl replied,
"Yes, but this is the first time I've seen one being reloaded!

In the Beginning....

Can you remember your earlier experiences of love and new relationships? Every new relationship starts with *limerance*, the early feelings of exhilaration, titillation, and high expectations. Limerance exudes sexuality and excitement, doesn't it? You anticipate the heart throbs, the fluid exchanges, and the revealing conversations. Limerance happens early in relationships, fortunately at any age too.

Uh oh! The limerance dance dies all too quickly.

Why?

You are in the relationship for a while when you begin perceive periods of loss. You might feel the loss of intensity, passion, love, sensuality, and even sexuality. What do you do, because it happens to all of us eventually?

Although that projection might be faulty, we feel it. That's the beginning... the wellbeing that we feel. Let's just take those feelings and put them in a box. Now those feelings are away in the box, and you've been in this relationship for a week, a month or one year or ten years.

I recommend that, as a start, you recall those earlier feelings of limerance. Remember, you can't reignite them (they've already burned brightly), but they can be remembered. The excitement that is inherent early in a relationship. You might capture the early feelings of passion, intensity, or sensuality in imagery: walking on the beach hand-in-love, making love on a quiet Sunday morning and then sharing a cup of coffee. Oh, and that delightful afterglow! With an image, you recapture feelings. Again, better yet, create new experiences and stories.

> *"Don't let the past remind us of what we are not now"* . . .
>
> —Crosby, Stills, Nash and Young

When the Thrill Is Gone

Suddenly, you look at the other person and think, "What the hell! What happened? I'm with you and I don't feel the same joy and excitement. I don't feel the same exhilaration. What is going on? What has changed?"

The mind craves for definitions. Even in the realm of love itself the mind demands analysts, discernment, and compartmentalization. The undefined needs to be defined. But once defined, it is no longer what it is. The definition itself obliterates the reality of what already is. That is a very simple, yet totally complicated question. Remember the first step is: to revisit and rekindle those old dance feelings by recalling what it was that drew you to this person originally. Pull out the box and look at the pictures in your head. Even if it was a mirage or a fantasy, what was it that really attracted you?

But now, it is time to incorporate loyalty, acceptance, commitment, and integrity into the mix. That's a mouthful, indeed! Truly, there is no other way to go. Merely recalling doesn't do it. Pretending or make-believe doesn't do it. Denial doesn't do it. And even ending the relationship doesn't do it!

> *Top Ten President Clinton Tips for Keeping the Romance in Your Marriage:*
>
> *10. Make sure every hundredth woman you sleep with is your wife.*
> *9. No matter how tasty it looks, don't eat her lipstick.*
> *8. Buy her FTD's 'Sorry About My Many Affairs' bouquet.*
> *7. Remember, your kisses taste sweeter when your mouth is full of donuts.*
> *6. Renew each other's membership in the Air Force One "Mile-High Club."*
> *5. Take Paula Jones off your speed dial.*
> *4. Keep gaining weight until each of your thighs is the size of that dreamy Leonardo DiCaprio.*
> *3. Candle-lit dinner at local Hooters.*
> *2. Try not to preface sex with, 'All right, let's get this over with.'*
> *1. A little dab of ketchup behind each ear.*
>
> —David Letterman, *The Late Show*

The Myth of Unconditional Love

Ok fellow travelers. I am ready to shatter an old ideal, challenge the very icon of an intimate relationship, and probably lead you on a path of very uncomfortable honesty. So, let's jump in!

A false belief and expectation can be, and most likely is, a very subtle but deadly trap in any relationship.

We take our marriage vows seriously and literally. This is a wonderful thing. But, those vows, though profound and romantic, mean nothing if not followed up by lots of hard work, some heartache, and continuous fluidity, coupled with loyalty.

We speak of "unconditional love" in our partnership, yet we know that this is not true. This particular human experience is reserved at best for our children and our parents. We love them when they're good and we love them when they're bad. We would never consider divorcing our children (OK… maybe SOMETIMES!).

In all of our love relationships some violations are just unforgivable. Most of us store them away, hoping that we never have to use them to justify a termination of our precious relationship. But they stand ready!

So What's Forever?

What makes a relationship intimate and true is honesty. That's where it starts and stops. There is no philosophy or approach to relationships that guarantees longevity and permanence. Like many other gifts in life, all relationships are truly "one day at a time." Honesty, however, contributes highly to that longevity.

I have found that if I stay in the day, be aware and take responsibility for myself, and understand that my partner is *not* an appendage or extension of myself or my ego, then all is well.

Is a terminated relationship a failure? No, as long as you've learned something about <u>yourself</u> through the process. Because a relationship is ended does not eliminate or undo all the wonderful moments and experiences that were shared in that relationship.

> *Suddenly, I'm not half the man I used to be.*
> *There's a shadow hanging over me.*
> *Oh, yesterday came suddenly.*
>
> —Paul McCartney

Afterglow—Points to Remember

o   It is vital at this point in your journey that you realize that certain visual images and stories provoke and stimulate exciting and passionate feelings.

o   The relationship images that we have formulated, and their subsequent use as a schematic, benchmark or foundation for our real life relationships keep us miserably frustrated, morbidly disappointed, and undeniably imprisoned.

o   Throughout this book we're challenging the roles that make us feel captured and drive us to capture others. What we are learning to do is acknowledge them, define them, limit them, and yes, we're even going to play with them.

o   My invitation to you is to accept that you are whole and perfect. A truly intimate relationship makes you more so.

o   The real dance of intimacy is the music called change and diversity. Intimacy comes from your attitude and willingness, but also from your experiences.

o   A false belief (or strong immutable belief) and expectations can be, and most likely is, a very subtle but deadly trap in any relationship. Honesty, however, contributes highly to relationship longevity.

FEAR OF INTIMACY
DISTRUST
RESENTMENT
How can we make love with all of these strangers in bed with us?
DISAPPOINTMENT
JEALOUSY
Darling, they're NOT strangers... They're friends. Let them stay.
UNREASONABLE DEMANDS
ANGER

Chapter 8

A New Outlook for Intimacy

The process and joy of applying new ideas and more realistic expectations in our relationships.

The Look of Intimacy

I'm asked quite often how true intimacy looks. How does it feel and how does it play out? I find that most people expect true intimacy to feel like a dog-eared page from a romantic novel where the idyllic setting offers a quiet stroll through a field of flowers. With no bees! It's peaceful for romance, sensuality and the "merging of souls."

Oh, partners, if only it were true. That scenario captures your heart and leaves your mind in the imaginal realm somewhere.

Personal Love, however intense and well-meaning, eventually binds. It's very focus creates conflict and despair. It even creates disharmony because it intrinsically confines and demands.

In our real world, true intimacy looks quite different.

Expecting attachment and dependency upon another person to create love and compassionate is like expecting temporary satisfaction of desire to create happiness and peace. Kind of like screaming for silence, or fighting for peace.

Some of the most intimate moments between Keaw and ! are not at the height of sexual connection, and not during periods of agreement and sharing mutual contentment and satisfaction. Rather, intimate periods might be of one of us expressing our feelings directly without apology, explanation nor defense to the other.

Imagine putting the children to sleep, turning the lights low, tucking in the Guinea pig, and going to bed naked. Then gently touching your partner and allowing tears to stream from your eyes. There is no demand or expectation for relief from you and no expectation of explanation or defense from your partner.

This is the sign of true intimacy. Of course this could be a different realm of expression as joy, or contentment or frustration, or even anger (always to be tempered with sensitivity and kindness).

Even Anger?

Yes, the expression of intimacy could even be anger. Anger expressed in a trusting and intimate relationship does not have to be threatening and certainly not destructive. This is true as long as the source and the apparent or contrived reason for the anger is clear. Recrimination, justification and blame, coupled with anger, are always destructive. The anger itself is not.

It is tremendously important to find a way of expressing anger that is non-threatening and can be mutually empowering. This is a difficult concept for many people to understand because along with feelings of anger usually ride feelings of blame, aggression, fear, rejection and even self-pity. People associate anger with negative emotions and even death! It does not have to be that way.

Well, I get so mad, I stamp and shout,
I scream and yell, and I frown and pout,
Now this song is done and you've learned about bein' mad!!!
WAAAHHHHHHH!!!!

"Mad Song" Sesame Street

Anger Can Be Empowering!

Think for a moment of a two-year-old who's angry. When angry, she is not focused on the source of anger. Most likely, she doesn't know what it is; she hasn't connected her feeling with a particular event. All she experiences is rage at that particular moment.

We adults will ask children why they're angry and try to solve what we think is the problem quickly because it's disruptive— especially if it is in a public place. We want to end it; but the two-year-old is teaching us a lesson that the source of frustration, disappointment, abandonment or threat that initiated the anger does not matter. The anger itself is what's important, and two-year-olds know how to express it so well.

The toddler is teaching us that it is safe to express anger because he or she knows deep inside that anger does not drive away people who truly love them. A two-year-old has a temper tantrum with the knowledge and the confidence that when it is over, he or she will still be loved, fed, and sheltered, nurtured and even forgiven.

This, of course, is in a balanced and healthy home. Wouldn't that be nice!

Intimacy Is Real!

I am encouraging you to be real with your emotions. That means to be not afraid of how emotions feel, and not afraid to present them to others, especially your intimate partner.

When Keaw and I are making love, sometimes earlier on in the experience, when all the noise is stopped and my experience becomes meditative, she or I may start crying. We allow ourselves that moment of expression because we know that we are completely safe and truly accepted.

Imagine how shocked your partner would be if that happened without warning the next time you're making love! A simple emotional expression like this could elicit inquiry and fear. Are there some unresolved issues of unhappiness and discontent within the relationship? These become the concerns, and your partner wants to know, "Did I cause it? Can I fix it?"

Stop already!!

> *"When you're feeling sad, it's the thing to do*
> *when your stomach aches*
> *Or your heart aches, too*
> *If you're scared, or you're hungry, or not very dry*
> *It's all right to cry . . . . cry . . . cry . . . cry."*
>
> -"It's All Right to Cry" Sesame Street

Feelings—More is Always Better!

Once a relationship becomes fully trusting and sufficiently intimate, I allow my partner to express to me feelings that have built up during the day that are not personally directed at me. The feelings have nothing to do with our present experience, but have been put on hold through the day. Feelings, when acknowledged, do not give us a sense of strength; mostly they seem to support vulnerably and a sense of weakness.

Desire and cultivate vulnerability in an intimate and trusting relationship; keep in mind that in the "cruel world," vulnerability and sensitivity may be considered a weakness and can leave you feeling unprotected.

In other words, don't try this in the corporate boardroom, but I encourage all to try this at home!

Intimacy Is Expression and Acceptance

Joan was a sensitive young woman who grew up in an emotionally expressive household. She was in touch with her feelings and not afraid to express them. However, when she moved up the management ladder within a larger corporation, she was not pleased with a particular decision that affected her department. In the next management meeting, Joan spoke up strongly about her personal feelings regarding the decision. Her supervisor pulled her aside after the meeting and explained that the meeting was not the forum for her to express her emotions; that in this corporate culture, emotional truth is not the way we do it.

Joan's story represents a deeper principal: emotional expression is not the issue. Beneath the verbalization or expression of emotion is our own personal truth. It's where we truly live as an individual.

Intimacy is to share that truth with your partner, having built a relationship where one's own truth does not become an immediate threat to the partner or to the relationship.

- o At any particular moment, a partner's truth might be sadness, jubilation, grief, fear, anger or just about anything else.
- o Assume that feeling is paramount and real and let them express it freely and in safety.
- o During that expression, neither partner feels responsible for creating that feeling or responsible for relieving it.

That is a token and reflection of true intimacy: *To be able to say to another human being with calm and comfort that "I am very sad," and be respected by the other person to the degree that that sadness itself is acknowledged and accepted.*

To Thine Own Self Be True

In order for a relationship to truly grow, we've already discussed that the individuals in the relationship have to give themselves permission to grow. This necessitates having the courage to feel and to be and express who you truly are.

I consider this ability an advanced stage of human awareness: *to thine own self be true.* To know yourself is paramount to developing a relationship with another. Is this easy? Absolutely not.

Sharing without Fixing

True intimacy is sharing without needing to fix, rescue or change. My daughter was ill last night. Since she is in need of some surgery, I was feeling kind of raw this morning when I went to a self-help meeting.

In the meeting, they were talking about relationships and intimacy, and I started sharing, and then just cried for several minutes. My tears seemed to make some people uncomfortable. This is my way of experiencing sadness. I actually learned it from an episode of "Sesame Street" (intellectual giant that I am!). We all have our own ways.

Bert and Ernie were singing a song called "When I'm Itchy, I Scratch." My favorite lyrics were:

"Now, when I'm happy, I laugh. When I'm sad, I cry. I get my melons in the melon patch, and when I'm itchy, I scratch."

While listening to this song, I thought it was amazingly wise. So why do we make it hard as adults?

The Willingness to Allow Ourselves, and Others, to Be "Wrong"

Not putting energy behind proving a position or needing to be right is a critical skill and commitment when handling agreements and disagreements. It's critical to differentiate and to discern how to handle agreements in a true partnership, but also with one's relationship with the world.

People seem to have an instinctive need, when there is a lack of agreement on a certain point, to convince another that one's own position is correct and others are wrong.

At one time or another, we've engaged in this type of struggle with the world and with our partner: to defend our position or to prove our rightness.

The intimacy principle is that it's really not necessary to do so, and it is actually destructive.

Space Invasion

Have you noticed that there is an ongoing fear of a violation of space, whether physical, intellectual or conceptual space? An example of physical space violation in the last few decades is drivers maintaining and controlling their own road space. If that is violated, a driver may very well become belligerent and violent.

Take that principle of territory violation, apply it to the cognitive, emotional and spiritual dynamics in a relationship, and the same scenario is played over and over again.

I've seen couples argue over how to cook a roast, boil an egg, and make a bed, whether or not to make the bed, how to dress the children, how to load the dishwasher, whether or not to have children, whose house to visit this holiday, how to fold towels, and where to eat dinner.

Think about it, pilgrims. Is it really that big a deal? When the sun rises the next morning, is it that important to be right?

Gotta Be Right?

Personally, I would rather be happy than right. Let me run this up the flagpole and see who salutes it.

For some reason people feel that their opinion, even if based on their limited true experience, must be accurate. Duhhhh! This position and subsequent justification leads to disharmony and conflict in most relationships. The defending position doesn't have a sound basis in supporting intimacy within a relationship. If we dig our heels in at any point in the relationship, declare that our way is the only way, and further demand that our partner not only conform but agree with our way, we're headed for nothing but trouble.

Some of these declarations of power and control are subtle and some are quite direct. People pick out one statement, feel it's true for them, and then make it a brutal reality for everyone else. Even worse, they often make important decisions based on faulty reasoning that affects the partner. The battle lines are drawn. The gauntlet is thrown. Disharmony and failure is inevitable.

Surrender to Win

I think that all of us are capable of rationalizing and justifying whatever behavior we choose. We go on to create whole stories about it. We call our friends who certainly agree and support our indignation and self-righteous attitude.

It's even more amazing how partners often accept or defer to these positions rather than argue. Both positions are engaging and suffocating.

You are so captured when you passively surrender your truth.

Declare Wrong!

What is eminently necessary in avoiding contention when there is a failure to agree is for each to admit to the smallest possibility that they could be wrong. Come on, we can all do that! Start with this foundation of opinion, then the opinion does not become empowered and energized as a crusade. This is tremendously important.

Even in the heat of disagreement between Keaw and me, there is a necessity that we both apply and acknowledge: *in spite of our feeling of correctness, we could in fact be wrong.*

How does it feel to confess, admit or acknowledge that you could be wrong? Well if you're in the beginning of our common spiritual journey, it might be very threatening. It might be naturally distressing because we are trained to believe that we are right. So it's not a comfortable feeling. But it's a necessary one!

Agreeing to Disagree Without Resolution

However, it is important in relationship to avoid the need for continual resolution. Otherwise, instead of having one large war, we have skirmishes and battles continuously. These detract and defer us from the primary goal, which is trust, closeness and intimacy.

So, I am encouraging you . . .

o   Not to avoid differences,
o   Rather... acknowledge, verbalize and exchange differences,
o   Invest some degree of emotional expression in the interchange.

In intimacy, there isn't a need for a strong protective stance for your perspective. To do so is often diminishing and often fatal. Is that pretty clear?

How will you recognize it?

If You Just Can't Help Yourself

If your level of perceived emotional distress and psychic threat is so high as an apparent result of disagreement, then I suggest, just as I would to a two-year-old, that you take a time out. Back off, consider, and reconsider what you're feeling and what you feel it is being threatened and why whatever that is MUST be protected.

o   What is being threatened in this exchange?
o   Is it a question of bruised ego?
o   Do feelings of inadequacy surface in the process of deferment?
o   Are there real facts in real life that support the position?

Take responsibility for your feelings. Don't burden your partner with your own issues at this point.

Such an emotional charge in a disagreement calls for each side to become temporarily disconnected. Disengage consciously and mutually and use the tools you have to acknowledge and process emotion. The point is to discharge your energy in an informal and natural way if you stay with your intimate partner. You have a mutual "time out."

It's not that you mean to hurt, but hurt is usually the result of processing and expending this energy. Like setting off a stick of TNT, you may need to do that, but do it in a safe place. Anybody around is going to be injured.

Continuing that metaphor, if you're going to light a stick of dynamite, just make sure the area is clear before you light the fuse.

Share Responsibility

As partners in a committed, caring, intimate relationship, we have the same responsibility. I'm not saying that stick of dynamite doesn't exist. I'm not even saying that it doesn't have to explode.

I am saying if it is going to happen, clear the area. There is no excuse or justification to do it in a way that's going to be harmful or hurtful to another person.

Only after that charge and that power behind it are diminished, do I suggest that you continue the intimate dialogue.

The error that many people make is that they have to "unload" their feelings on who they mistakenly believe are the source of the problem, when truly it is us that create the problem!

The Threat of Honesty in a Relationship

Can honesty destroy a relationship? Absolutely!

However, please know that if honesty destroys a relationship, there's a very strong likelihood that it was never truly an intimate, committed or healthy relationship from the onset.

Why? The main ingredient of a truly intimate relationship *is* honesty, even when the honesty appears to hurt or disappoint the other person. We have learned in the prior chapter that newly formed relationships are usually replete with deception, which presents an enigma if one's objective is acceptance and endearment. This is probably a reasonable road to take in a relationship because if we were just completely bare, open and honest, we'd probably scare our partner away too soon. Let them love us <u>first</u>, and then we'll get real!

Got Commitment?

Relationships have a constant theme, and that is commitment between the partners. Deception, either by direct lies or by omission, needs to be slowly and consistently realized and eliminated. This is a straining and arduous (and unending) process, and requires both partners to agree to "hang in there."

One might be tempted to maintain a certain level of dishonesty, feeling that it's necessary to avoid conflict. One might conclude that if there doesn't seem to be any major conflict or disagreements, then the relationship is sound, solid and of great value. It doesn't.

I have personally seen many relationships that have been arrested at this level—continued 'til death did them part. You've probably seen them—the "living dead" of marriages. Ghostly mirages eat dinner together and stare into space apathetically. They silently mourn for extinguished passion.

So let's get on with the more lofty or difficult decision of committing to true intimacy and closeness in a relationship.

Ready, Set, Accept

True intimacy is closeness with complete (or at least 90%) honesty.

The dynamic of true intimacy is one of mutual exposure, disclosure, empathy, honesty, and finally, acceptance. Be forewarned, though. Acceptance does not eliminate conflict, or pain. It allows it.

That's really is the foundation of true intimacy.

To reiterate, honesty can be difficult because it is very uncomfortable. We know that honesty is especially difficult to share with another person when we're not really honest with ourselves from the beginning.

> *"Real isn't how you are made," said the Skin Horse. "It's a thing that happens to you. When a child loves you for a long, long time, not just to play with, but really loves you, then you become Real."*
> *"Does it hurt?" asked the Rabbit.*
> *"Sometimes," said the Skin Horse, for he was always truthful. "When you are Real you don't mind being hurt."*
>
> *—The Velveteen Rabbit* by Margery Williams

Pop Quiz: *How Do You Lie to Yourself?*

DO I (TRUE/FALSE):

o   Say "I'll deal with it later."
o   Suppress feelings until my gut is full and screams at me.
o   Keep quiet, telling myself it's for the better, to keep the peace, etc.
o   Tell myself that I shouldn't tell my truth because it will hurt his/her feelings.
o   Convince myself not to be honest because it jeopardizes my security.
o   Tell myself that I really don't care, when I really do.
o   Tell myself that s/he is too good for me and might leave, explode, or do something stupid, so I'd better to just keep quiet.

Why Be Honest?

We've all seen people who abuse honesty, where someone makes a statement that is ill-timed, has a negative tone, or a feeling of hostility: *I'm just being honest with you. I'm telling you this for your own sake. I want you to be aware of this. This will make our relationship stronger. You need to know this. I can't ignore this anymore; what I have to say is . . .*

Honesty is no excuse for aggression. Never accept that.

In intimacy, honesty has to be tempered with some empathy and sensitivity to the other person. Honesty is vital, but the timing really needs to be right.

People often use honesty, either purposely or inadvertently, as retribution. It's not that anger should be eliminated. It needs to be expressed with compassion.

It's similar to what people typically do with sarcasm. You and I know that sarcasm is a backhanded way to attack and express a negative opinion or criticism about another person. Then we cloak it in fun and make a joke out of it like good-natured teasing. That's an ineffective, offensive and pointless way of communicating, and quite hurtful.

Captured! This way of communicating doesn't support a true exchange, and it doesn't allow for a process of conflict resolution. Everybody becomes defensive.

You're capturing the other person with your anger, and it's a harsh capture. It's a hostile capture, not leaving any room for any kind of peace talks. There's no way out. You've created a situation with no option because the situation itself is deceptive and hurtful..

Dance Lightly

Like honesty can destroy a bad relationship, dishonesty can destroy a good one. There might be a desire or tendency to dance around issues and agree to stay away from certain topics and issues. This is known as the "no talk rule." Let's *stay shallow so we don't have to deal and experience real issues in our relationship.* Many people do this, not only in relationships, but in life in general..

Facing My Honesty Quiz

How I deal with honesty (yes/no):

Do I just follow along blindly?
Do I change your mode of conversation—become more intellectual?
Do I agree (conspire) not to address the issue?
Can I talk around it?
Do I feel that I don't need to work at it any more (it'll go away)?
Do I tap dance as a distraction (make jokes, talk about the weather)?
Do I look up at the sky, go, "Wow! The sky is falling" and exit stage right?

If you answered yes to any of the above, then chances are your relationship is either dying or it's already dead. Are you preparing for funeral services? Change and life will be miraculously restored!

Are you ready for a true test of your honesty and commitment? Try this one on:

The "I Hate You" Principle

The "I Hate You Principle" can actually enhance your relationship.

Once in the great expanse called time, some of us, because of a "chemical imbalance," general genetic misfortune, or bad potty-training, feel intense antagonism and separation from the world and the people in it. I am one of them.

Sometimes I truly feel that the entire world is against me. This doesn't make any sense and, even as a feeling, is totally irrational. However, it is a true, honest, real feeling. I'm sure that high doses of fourth-generation anti-depressant medication would probably relieve me of that feeling, but it would probably relieve me of a lot of other vital feelings at the same time, including over thirty five years of sobriety!

So, to get back to what appears to be the problem—sometimes intense, deeply feeling people easily and quite naturally make their partner their enemy.

From The Mind

Here is how it looks in my world: So, I'm having a bad hair day. Everybody's against me; poor me; nobody understands me. I don't have any heroes and nobody is coming to my rescue. Then I get a call from Keaw and she asks me to pick up a gallon of milk. Keaw doesn't know that she is now my enemy. She has joined a gazillion-billion other people, and she's on the other side. She has the audacity to make a small request of me; she's crossed the line. The request now becomes a burden. At that moment, just like a two-year-old would, I feel, if not hatred, tremendous animosity and separation from Keaw, just as I do everybody else.

I could blame it on mommy and daddy. They told me that however I felt was wrong. Waaa! If I verbalized my feelings, they corrected me: "You don't really feel that way, do you?" Well, after years of this, I'd nod and say, "Uh? No? Am I right?"

What did I learn and what am I acting out irrationally? Most ways that kids learn to handle feelings include deferment, defining, denying, confining, or hiding. Many of us learn that we certainly cannot express our feelings to anybody else, certainly not to our partner. That would be fatal.

You *Must* Express in a Committed Relationship

My fellow sufferers… Here is a CLUE for you…

How you feel at any particular moment DOES NOT reflect who you are, or what you are. It is merely what you FEEL! And if those around you are repelled, confused, and upset over what you are feeling, WHO is truly responsible for their upset?

When the world is against you, and your partner irrationally appears to be in the enemy camp, just say, "I hate you." State it with as much bile and vehemence as you wish and be done with it.

Why is it safe to do this? You and your partner worked it out beforehand so each of you has an escape hatch for the steaming emotions. You've already agreed to:

- Be aware of the venting (expressing) that needs to happen.
- Know that your partner's feelings are all about him/her, and not about you.
- Don't take it personally; it's just your partner's volcano spewing a little or a lot.
- Your partner's statement of "hating you" at that particular moment does not negate in any way, the value, continuity, commitment, affection or even love within the relationship. I cannot stress enough how vitally important this is!

The mind is ALWAYS in movement. That is it's very nature, and dynamic. From the mind, sometimes appearing to be instantaneous, are feelings that are generated not only from the present experience, but from an avalanche of memories (both recalled and forgotten), and from anticipation of the future, also based on the past. In other words… the snake chasing his (or hers) own tail!

Feelings 101 (for those who missed Mister Rogers)

To some degree or another, all of us experience feelings that appear to be inappropriate, threatening, or are contrary to the desired consistency or perceived demands of a relationship. Those demands may be from our partner, or very well may be from ourselves!

In summary,

- You have your feelings.
- They're your feelings alone.
- They're not a threat to your commitment in an intimate relationship.
- They're just your feelings. I promise! They flow.

If you are honest about your feelings, and you can be intimate and share them with your partner, you have done your job and met your responsibility in the relationship. If your partner takes your feelings as a threat to your commitment, or your blatant honesty scares them, then THEY need to work through that, not you!

As a matter of fact, if you jump in and deny the honesty of what you are feeling or felt, you are in fact culpable in the deterioration of the very relationship you want to support.

Many newcomers to the realm of intimacy misinterpret the honest expression of feelings as an indicator of a relationship violation, or even failure! The battle cry goes, "If you really loved me, you wouldn't feel that way." OUCH! I'm trapped!

Enhance Intimacy

There is an ugly rumor circulating that feelings are not fact. This is far from the truth. Feelings are often more fact that thoughts, concepts and cognitive perceptions. They happen, and are often stronger than the thoughts that they are based on.

Feelings must be acknowledged, honored, and valued. People need to give themselves and each other permission to experience and share a whole range of feelings at the same time. It's all dynamic, and it's often unpredictable. We are affected not only by environment, but also by internal chemistry, genetics, cheeseburgers and all kinds of weird and wonderful things. One moment we feel love, adoration and acceptance of another person, and then the next moment, a feeling of hostility, fear, or contempt comes up. That's not crazy. That's human.

Feelings aren't Jack-in the-boxes. You can't push down a feeling when it pops up. You need to embrace it or accept it instead. Feelings are internal gauges; they have no direct relationship to the quality of your partnership. They are internally produced, not a response to some deficiency or violation of the partner. Honor your inner life.

Sharing feelings, without contempt or some other motive, with your lover is a tremendous indicator of maturity and intimacy in the relationship.

If you feel separate, misunderstood, unappreciated, undervalued, or alone for a period of time with your lover, don't panic, and again, do try this at home.

Your Humanness Enhances Your Relationship

You're being offered an opportunity to reaffirm your true commitment to your relationship. The intimacy goal is to mutually accept and experience elements of life that are part of our natural humanness.

In loving one, you love all. In loving all, you love each. One and all are not exclusive. You will realize this when you understand that love is not a doing. It is a being.

Relationships don't shelter us from experiencing all that the world has confronted us with. Real partners don't rescue us from the hurt of the world—or the hurt and emptiness we carry inside.

Being with another person does not relieve us of feeling lonely or feeling alone.

But it should always offer us the priceless gift of sharing all of these feelings and experiences with another. And knowing that, through it all, we are accepted for who and what we are.

Afterglow—Points to Remember

o   Anger expressed in a trusting and intimate relationship does not have to be threatening and certainly not destructive.

o   I encourage you to be real with your thoughts and emotions. That means to be not afraid of how emotions feel, and not afraid to present them to others,

o   Intimacy is to share that personal truth with your partner, having built a relationship where one's own transient truth does not become an immediate threat to the partner or to the relationship

o   I consider this ability an advanced stage of human awareness: *"to thine own self be true"*. And also to your partner!

o   Not putting energy behind proving a position or needing to be right is a critical skill and commitment when handling agreements and disagreements.

o   To avoid contention when there is a failure to agree is for each to admit to the smallest possibility that they could be wrong.

o   The constant and immutable theme in relationships is commitment between the partners.

o   The dynamic of true intimacy is one of mutual exposure, disclosure, empathy, honesty, and finally, acceptance. Be forewarned, though. Acceptance does not eliminate conflict, or pain. It allows it.

o   If you are honest about your feelings, and you can be intimate and share them with your partner, you have done your job and met your responsibility in the relationship. Both to your partner, and yourself. The two are ALWAYS inter-related!

UNIBROW
OBVIOUS COMB-OVER
GAP-TEETH
PIMPLES
ENORMOUS EARS
TRUE LOVE!
FLABBY ARMS
BELLY-BUTTON LINT
ANCIENT TIGHTY WHITIES
SPARE-TIRE
KNOBBY KNEES
SIGH

Chapter 9

Learning from Our Past Mistakes

Eliminating the compromises that we make to others and ourselves in our relationships.

Imagine the Possibility

Imagine the options if intimate partners could really communicate honestly and forthrightly with each other.

o You could be so honest with an intimate and confess to them truly that you are not full. You could look them in the eye and say, "I'm with you, and I still don't feel complete."
o You could say exactly how you feel, not have to qualify it, justify it, realign it, or make it more palatable or less threatening with a dance of words.
o You could say anything, any way you desire to voice it, even though it might cause distress. Can you be comfortable with the uncomfortable?

What stands in our way of being completely honest? Most of us don't realize that the meat of the message doesn't matter. *How* you convey the message does matter.

It isn't what you say; it is how and why you say it. That's the real potential problem.

Get Beyond It

How can we get beyond that? When people regard and value each other, the wisdom of their shared human experiences, whether joyful or painful are always productive. If we accept this without feeling threatened, then we are certainly on track.

In an intimate partnership, the trust between you and your lover creates a safe network for communication and acceptance. Each should be able to speak anything and still be okay with each other. Partners need to know that they don't walk out of the room and a relationship is not terminated when one's sensitivity is offended. Each must trust the other to not violate his/her sensitivity, and if feeling violated, to know that the intimate connection carries both hearts through any turmoil.

This is often hard to understand because your mind continues to process events as "me" or "them" events. This is destructive and non-sequitur in a vital living relationship. Although I think that I've made it clear that two people in a relationship do NOT merge into one, you need to be aware that the mind plays tricks, constantly, In most instances of thought processing, it is ONLY working from the "ME" perspective, not the "US" perspective.

A husband and wife were having dinner at a very fine restaurant when an absolutely stunning young woman comes over to their table, gives the husband a big kiss, tells him she'll see him later, and walks away. His wife glares at him and says, "Who was that??!!"

"Oh" replies the husband, "that was my mistress."

"That's it," says the wife, "I want a divorce." "Ok," replies her husband, "but remember, if you get a divorce there will be no more shopping trips to Paris, no wintering in the Caribbean, no Lexus in the garage, and no more country club. But, the decision is yours."

continued

> *Just then the wife notices a mutual friend entering the restaurant with a gorgeous woman. "Who is that woman with Jim?" she asks. "That's his mistress," replies her husband.*
>
> *"Oh. We have much better taste. Ours is much better looking." says the wife.*

The Ideal

People, stand true, naked, and accept each other. Be spontaneous, be comfortable, and have no need for any mask, script or story. Do not be captured by other people's reactions, demands or expectations.

The Opportunity

Deep down, the opportunity this book represents is for you to have intimacy without surrender. That means not being captured by subtle but profound reactions we have when we are truly genuine, and by the words we choose, or the way we present ourselves. That is the controlling, defining and confining experience. And we don't want that, compadres!

The Truth about Partner Choices

The choice of the particular "person" in a relationship is really secondary to the content of that relationship. The most important ingredients you add to a relationship are commitment, your willingness to be honest, your time and risk to expose <u>your</u> vulnerability.

All this stuff that feels so uncomfortable is the meat and potatoes of a relationship. To carry on that metaphor, it's not the bowl in which you put it. The contents of the bowl are important; the bowl itself is irrelevant.

Intimate relationships all boil down to your commitment, which is followed by all these acts of courage and bravery. These acts of courage and bravery are the process of true intimacy. It always is. It has little to do with the other person. Never has. Never will.

So What Stands in Our Way?

How do we fit together? One problem is that we don't fit each other's criteria list. If you think a certain way, then you and I can't hop in the sack together and have a little fun. Why? You may close the door mentally to such an experience because you believe I have a particular element, belief or a style that would not be a "fit" for you.

This might even be reflected by past experience. For example, your second husband was a staunch Republican, and he ended up running away with his 27-year-old blonde secretary. To insure that doesn't happen again, you see to it that the next husband is not a staunch Republican. Or even worse, you decide to distrust all men forever.

Not to bore you again with an important detail about the mind... It thrives on taking emotional memories (especially "negative" ones), replaying them, projecting them into the future, and taking amazing steps NOT to re-experience them. So consider yourself bored, but awakened!

Yes, it is illogical and based upon a skewed belief that closes the door to further intimacy and understanding of self and the partner. Being a staunch Republican has nothing to do with running away with a 27-year-old blonde secretary. Being a deceitful horny-dog has to do with that. Maybe what you need is someone who isn't so thwarted, shallow, or unwilling to share some of their fantasies with you.

Married life is full of excitement and frustration:

- *In the first year of marriage, the man speaks and the woman listens.*
- *In the second year, the woman speaks and the man listens.*
- *In the third year, they both speak and the neighbors listen.*

The connection that people make between personality, beliefs and even emotional expression, and figuring that they can sort all that out before they even engage in the preliminary parts of a relationship in order to avoid later disappointment, is absolutely—outrageously silly!

The Inherent Danger of a Closed System

A closed system is a relationship where there's no diversity in the intimacy. The relationship, in a very disarming and unexpected way, becomes spiritually and emotionally incestuous

One of the complaints in a committed relationship is a sense of boredom. Though it sounds paradoxical, we can create rituals to offset this boredom.

Rituals can run the gamut from the physical to the spiritual. For example, in the morning, Keaw and I have a ritual about getting up and being quiet, almost meditative. I rise first, go downstairs, and make the coffee and bagels. I set the table. She gets up slowly, checks in with Jennifer Juniper (our young daughter) and wanders downstairs. We have soft light on, no noise, and we sit there and enjoy our silence in shared space, and share that joy with our child. Our physical ritual is comforting to all of us. So, this is fine.

However, beware! Many people engage in various other rigid and myopic rituals that are intellectual or cognitive, and are also emotionally and spiritually draining. I believe the latter are the most threatening to continued intimacy and honesty within a relationship.

Why?

Well, having and expressing specific feelings becomes acceptable and expected. It becomes almost like a puzzle with an established framework that defines the patterns. There is no new expression, only the same framework to your emotional expression.

You never want to get out of that framework because there can be confusion, maybe misunderstanding, and even hurt, disappointment or anger.

The framework seems to be a nice way of creating and maintaining a close relationship. To put it in metaphoric terms, you have built your house, furnished it, and demand that nothing be changed. Comfort often breeds dissatisfaction.

You know what to expect. You know what "the score" is. You know what's acceptable—you know what's not. You know what hurts your partner, what makes your partner feel good and bad. Once you know the ground rules of the framework, you stay within it and don't stray. Sounds idyllic, right? Or, even on a good day, uninspiring!

Out of the Boundaries: Then—kaboom! One morning, one of you wakes up and realizes that you are bored: this day is going to be the same as yesterday and last week. With the discomfort of breaking the agreed upon boundaries, maybe one of you shares it with another. Boundaries are broken, and you feel trapped and confused. This, in fact, shows potential.

Ritual is good, and it gives people a comfort zone. But when you are suffocated by it, and there's no diversity and spontaneity, then it becomes a closed system. It is a closed system in that there's no additional experience, or new energy from outside the system.

Sparks of Spontaneity: In a self-contained system there are few sparks of spontaneity. There is a spiritual principle: if you close off from the rest of the universe, then you're cutting off energy and possibilities. If you do that, even in a strongly committed, intimate relationship, then your intimacy suffocates. It lacks air and all the other nutrients for growth. These nutrients cannot be produced internally for they stem from diversity and the very universe that we live in!.

> *The only charm of marriage is that it makes a life of deception necessary for both parties.*
>
> —Oscar Wilde

Captured Victim

To boredom and boundaries, people typically respond: "Gee, we've run this relationship out. I'm bored. I'm afraid to break out of the ritual and the framework that we've created, so let's just dump it. Let me just dump you, and start with someone else."

Pointing the Finger(s): Linda is a serial monogamist. She has a history of finding and discovering fault in her partner. She uses it repeatedly as justification to terminate her committed relationships. Linda states that a specific violation, especially a violation of fidelity, which means that she can never trust that particular person again. She makes that statement complete, total and fatal, as many women do.

Linda defines her values and lives by them stringently. And, of course, judges and rejects others accordingly.

Linda points the finger, and while it may be justified, Linda also has to take responsibility for the creation of intimate communication and clarity around the issue. However, as I asked previously, is this possible with Linda's closed mind and sharp boundaries?

To some degree or another, whether we make that violation tangible by behavior, we always have some degree of violation internally. As an example, you have sworn and vowed to monogamy, and while you are walking with your wife in the shopping mall, some cute 22-year-old gives you a good smile and a wiggle. Now we know there may be a pleasurable response to that particular experience. If not, check your pulse and make sure you're still alive!

Is that pleasurable response a violation of fidelity? No, and here is one place where we can draw some boundaries. I think it unnatural and unreasonable to restrict the use of our imagination and the natural human desire to fantasize and visualize.

Fantasize: I encourage you to share fantasies with your partner as the basis for a long-term intimate relationship. Our willingness to share in this realm is a vital element in trust and intimacy.

I am suggesting that you share those secret fantasies, however outlandish, unreasonable and unattainable they may be. There is no threat posed by presenting these to one's partner if the partnership is truly committed.

All these little secret ideas that blossom are not nearly as threatening as you might think they would be. Such does not demonstrate diminished affection, sensitivity or commitment to the other person.

Au contraire, if you get to this point in your relationship, consider it an indicator that you are on the right road to true intimacy. Enjoy, baby, enjoy!!

When a newly married man looks happy, we know why.
But when a ten-year-married man looks happy, we wonder why.

Limerize: "Wow, like I don't even feel my emptiness anymore." "You make me whole; you are my soul mate, the answer to my prayers, my meal-ticket." "I want to have your baby." "I want you to have my babies."

Sound familiar in the courtship rituals? A new partner lulls us into believing that all painful feelings and negative life experiences are healed and will remain that way. This is called the Limerance Stage, which can be detrimental if you fall for it, and wonderfully sexy if you can just enjoy it. Let me explain—where does that limerance thinking come from?

Father Knows Best? The Simpson's? The Soprano's? Reality TV?

Yes! That's exactly where our false expectations of intimacy came from, because we never see or come to accept our real life. We never see the empty spaces between the laugh tracks.

I was thinking about situation comedies this morning. What if the story lines and drama trauma were replayed in our own living room and bedroom? We would not be laughing because the realness of the multidimensional human drama would have more meaning to us personally.

In other words, what we find so humorous are reflections of our own weaknesses, constant childish demands, and anticipation and expectations of a "brighter future".

You say we'll soar like two birds through the clouds
But soon you'll cage me on your shelf
I'll never learn to be
Just me first, by myself.
That's the Way I Always Heard It Should Be

By Carly Simon and Jacob Brackman.

Once the soul mate feeling vanishes, can I share my terror, my loneliness or my discouragement with my lover without threatening them or feeling that I've betrayed them? That's the Cosmic Dilemma and challenge.

Emotional Codependency

To say, "What I **need** from a relationship is not coming from this particular person, so let me go to another person," is pure codependency. You seek a relationship, based upon fulfillment of your perceived needs. Zapped! You surrendered and are about to be eaten by intimacy ignorance. An insatiably hungry zombie monster!

You're using another human being to cure something they have nothing to do with—your perceived needs.

Sexual Inadequacy: Leonard and Lucy have been married four years and love each other deeply. Lately, Leonard has been thinking of "swinging". That is, he fantasizes about he and Lucy having sex with another married couple. It is incongruous with his whole idea of fidelity, yet he wonders how he might perform sexually with another woman. Would he be more excited? Would she find him to be amorous? Does he dare broach the subject with Lucy? Would he ever know if he can sexually please another woman?

He feels his relationship with Lucy is truly intimate, yet he cannot bring himself to speak of his fantasy. She might take it the wrong way? Leonard and Lucy have specific pictures of what each has to do to be acceptable, lovable, romantic and sexual.

Somewhere along the line, Lucy and Leonard have been lulled into believing that things had to be a certain way in order to get and maintain certain important things in life. And if we could just be that way, then things would be okay. And if you're not, you're in trouble, and don't let your partner find out about it.

Just Do It: What about just being honest? Communicating? Stepping out the closed thinking loop and risking that your partner loves you enough to understand?

How do you break out of that prison? Can you even believe that you've been deceived? You've been misdirected? You've been too insulated?

All this information separated you from your own humanness and has created a tremendous gulf between you and your true nature. You present yourself as you are expected to be, not how you truly are.

Hitting the Core Fear: Try this one on! If you present yourself as you are, you will not get your needs met, nobody will love you, nobody will respect you, everybody will criticize you, and you'll live and die a lonely and despondent death. In pure isolation, because you're not playing the game, you're not wearing the right clothes, you're not saying the right things, you're not driving the right car, you're not choosing the right career, you're not doing all these things that have been told to you.

However, you realize that you followed all of the rules, but are still getting bad results and feel an undeniable emptiness deep within. Ouch!

You only have one choice for true intimacy: Be real, authentic, honest and committed. These common principles are applied in different ways, to different degrees, with different people, and their applications are valid, worthwhile and effective.

Do we want it? You betcha baby! Just claim it NOW!

When to Dump Your Partner (Or... "I Should Have Done That YEARS Ago!")

Throughout this book, we're been talking about how to rescue and enhance your primary relationship. However, there are times when it is appropriate, and absolutely necessary, to end the relationship. When is this?

The short answer to this question is if your partner is cruel, physically abusive or evil. Dump the partner. Waste no time!

This sounds so simple, doesn't it? We expect that everybody would know to dump an abusive partner. But I also can imagine someone being in a physically or emotionally abusive relationship and trying to fix it, or even apparently enjoying it!.

There are occasions where terminating a relationship should not take a lot of time, retrospection or a wake-up call.

People in abusive relationships get confused because they know they feel uncomfortable, but don't always know the reason why. They don't understand what's inside that's making them feel discomfort because they don't know what's inside. They have no clue.

So it doesn't feel right or good, but what does that mean? Nothing, other than it doesn't feel right or good.

Script: Enter stage right a schoolteacher who is a naïve, loving, honest, sweet girl. She falls in love with this guy who marries her and they have one child. The guy is having affairs on her. She doesn't know it.

This guy confides to his friend that he and his wife go to counseling because wifey-dear feels something is missing. Sound familiar? He continues to tell his friend that he is going to get his wife pregnant because she loves being a mom. This keeps her happy and gives him the latitude he needs.

This is abusive, dishonest, and violates all principles of sensitivity and intimacy.

The Bottom Line

Draw the line in the sand to determine your boundaries, and then ask yourself if the demands or manipulations of a relationship interfere with other vital needs. If this is the case, the relationship should at least temporarily be ended. I think that's pretty clear if any aspect of the relationship:

- o threatens your life
- o makes it unsafe
- o causes risks to children or property.

Maybe part of this doesn't necessarily have to be a permanent commitment to dump; but if you require safe harbor, it is your responsibility to find that harbor. That's paramount.

Maybe the threat requires the need to get away or requires some sort of self-protection. Don't even think about it. Act on your knowing.

I don't want people stuck and saying, "Gee, there's got to be a way to work this out," and start trying to go steps of reparation when there is no way. When the partner is so far off, threatening, selfish and potentially hurtful that there is no conciliation, then get away fast and get safe.

Only in a position of safety can you start exploring yourself and your options.

Afterglow—Points to Remember

- In an intimate partnership, the trust between you and your lover creates a safe network for communication and acceptance. Each should be able to speak anything, and partners can continue to be okay with each other.
- This book encourages intimacy without surrender. That means not being captured by profound, subtle reactions that we have to exposing ourselves, the words we choose, or the way we present ourselves.
- You only have one choice for true intimacy: Be real, authentic, honest and committed. And be your own best friend!

Hey, FINALLY, our outfits DON'T clash!

Chapter 10

The Principles of Intimacy

Creating and applying new techniques to enhance our relationships.

Celebrating Individuality through Partnership

Of course you want to be loved and appreciated for your intellect and high standards. But how about being appreciated for having a cute butt and nice cleavage, a hairy chest and great biceps, good posture, or just being a wonderful sexual and sensual playmate? How about being valued for someone who can relax and truly enjoy being yourself and being with another person? Is this demeaning? NO!

> *"All of me, why not take all of me*
> *Can't you see I'm no good without you?*
> *Take these arms, I want to lose them*
> *Take these lips, I'll never use them."*
>
> *All of Me* by Louis Armstrong

Hold on to your seats. We're going to explore sex, a part of intimacy that is grossly misunderstood and often over, or under-valued.

And Then There Was Sex!

Our views of sexuality and intimacy are paradoxical because we often end up in a closed system, captured in society's media myths or someone else's script. We can lose our own sense of values and natural instincts. We lose sight of our apparent and seemingly quite real sexual needs and the value of physical connection whether it is touching or passionate love-making. We must remember that our bodies are avenues for us to communicate with our intimate partner and a wonderful way to express ourselves and bring pleasure to another. I want you to remember the excitement and playfulness that you can enjoy in your sexual relationships.

Sexuality, sensuality, desire and passion are simply part of our nature. Irrespective of sexual activity or degrees to which we manifest our passion into the world, they are streams within an endless power source that flow through us – this is merely what life is. When we deny or repress our own sexuality, we disconnect from our purity and nature, and from the magnificence of the living energies that are moving through us. Non-acknowledgement does not result in purity, nor does mere abstinence. Like many other things in life, it is understanding that is so important whether or not we choose to acknowledge and accept them.

There's no reason to list the myriad of thoughts and opinions on the subject of sexuality. We encounter and are trapped by them all the time. Each time you surrender unwittingly or knowingly to other people's opinions and values, you are *so* captured.

Let's set you free!

What's Good for the Goose

The point is to know *your* values. Is sexuality becoming a primary definition or standard in your relationship? Women, is this true of you? Men, do you bargain and continually seek for your penis' joy?

Here is a fun "sexuality quiz" for your edification and enjoyment:

When you get into bed next to partner at night, you are typically wearing:

- o   A flannel robe, heavy pajamas and a silly night hat.
- o   A silky shortie and intoxicating perfume.
- o   Nothing.

The kids are at a sleepover, and your spouse suggests renting a racy movie. You:

- o   Choose to rent an old John Wayne movie.
- o   You state categorically that you'd rather watch CNN.
- o   You remark, "Why rent one when we can make one."

It's a regular workday with nothing special going on. The underwear you have on is:

- o   BVDs with heavy waistband.
- o   Tie-dye underwear that was custom-made for no special occasion.
- o   None.

When you walk into the room, everyone knows you've arrived by your scent. You smell like:

- o   Janitor in a Drum, with a hint of 30-weight motor oil!
- o   Johnson's Baby Powder and Listerine
- o   Intoxicating. Your perfume lingers provocatively.

Sometimes your guy just doesn't seem to know his way around your body in bed. You:

- o   Draw a map of your erogenous zones, and place it over the headboard.
- o   Wiggle around, and even laugh or moan to give good hints.
- o   Put his hand and tongue in the right place, and then grin and bear it!

Your art class is studying the human form and needs a nude model. You:

- o   Quit the class, how disgusting!
- o   Try to rationalize how a naked body could be nonsexual.
- o   Volunteer, and bare all to your fellow artists, with a smile, naturally.

Your partner is out of town on a business trip, and wants to spice up the phone calls. When he calls, you:

- o   Protest, and inform him that you have dishes to wash!
- o   Realize that you have little or no creativity in this arena, and start reading excerpts from the Weekly World News.
- o   You say things that you've never said before.

Whew, was that a tough test! As before, there really are no right answers—this is just "food for thought." However, if you picked answer "3" to all the questions, I you and I need to talk. You are my hero!!!!

"The Test

A man is dating three women and wants to decide which to marry. He decides to give them a test. He gives each woman a present of $5000 and watches to see what they do with the money.

The first does a total makeover. She goes to a fancy beauty salon, gets her hair done, new makeup and buys several new outfits and dresses up very nicely for the man. She tells him that she has done this to be more attractive for him because she loves him so much. The man was impressed.

The second goes shopping to buy the man gifts. She gets him a new set of golf clubs, some new gizmos for his computer, and some expensive clothes. As she presents these gifts, she tells him that she has spent all the money on him because she loves him so much. Again, the man is impressed.

> *The third invests the money in the stock market. She earns several times the $5000. She gives him back his $5000 and reinvests the remainder in a joint account. She tells him that she wants to save for their future because she loves him so much. Obviously, the man was impressed.*
>
> *The man thought for a long time about what each woman had done with the money, and then he married the one with the biggest tits.*

The Challenge of Being Sexual

The fact is, we are all sexual beings whether we acknowledge it or not. Regarding displaying and enjoying our sexuality, we tend to choose one of three different approaches:

Choice 1: Sexuality is threatening, sinful, and self-indulgent. If I become sexual, if I engage in a sexual relationship with someone, at sometime, without the benefit of marriage, I'm demeaning myself. Society says that I've lowered my value as a person. I equate being sexual without an adequate story or justification to being promiscuous, loose, and having a low moral standard. And, of course, this must reflect low self-esteem and/or lack of self respect.

Choice 2: I recognize and acknowledge the value of my sexuality, and use that value (as it is perceived by others) to control and capture. Ouch!

Choice 3: My sexuality is mine to offer, enjoy, and experience. I have a defined set of standards that are personal and unique and I feel comfortable when I honor those standards. My sexual integrity is a reflection of my own set of values, not those of others.

Truth or Dare

The paradox is that if you "surrender" yourself sexually (without a promise, story or objective), you feel demeaned and worthless. On the other hand, if you don't, you feel that your relationship is lacking in depth. Then there are those who use sex as a tool of manipulation and control. That's never okay.

Each time you surrender your standards, compromise your perceived needs or sensitivities unwittingly, or use surrender or "favors" to manipulate others, you are fully engaged in the capturing process.

You need to stop, examine and analyze what it is that you truly value in yourself. What you value most, others will also most value. If, in fact, it's not your sexuality, then why use sexuality as a tool or token of exchange? Why use it as a bargaining chip or as a means of controlling other people's behavior and level of commitment? You know you are much more, and have much more to offer. Don't diminish yourself!

Your Natural Value as an Individual

Appreciate yourself and value all your elements. Because you value your body and sexuality doesn't mean that you devalue yourself.

Because you like to show off your beautiful shoulders doesn't mean that you don't have a good head above them. Valuing yourself and your assets is another important principle of intimacy.

The Trophy Syndrome

At any particular time, if your partner is enjoying a certain part of your being, even to the extent of showing off and acting as if you are a "trophy" or an extension of his or her ego and value, enjoy it! Go along for the ride. Why not lighten up and say, "Okay, this is just a body part. If my partner is especially proud of my whole body, let's celebrate this together! Let's show off! Go dancing, play pool (with your butt way sticking out while you're making that hard shot), circulate, and get some needed attention!

People are often threatened by this concept because of lack of self-confidence, and misinformation. This whole idea of a trophy demonstrates the concept that one person in the relationship being an extension of their partner. Just as a Jaguar XKE is often viewed as an extension of a man's penis, so might a huge kitchen with a triple oven, granite countertops, and triple chrome refrigerator be a reflection of a woman's ability to nurture or provide comfort for a family.

Yes, we know that this is ludicrous and is not really reflective of one's true ability whether it is penis size or cooking talent. However, this is how our thoughts connect the dots between penis and Jaguar—by association.

o   What trophy pictures do you have in your head?
o   What trophy scenarios do you act out with your intimate partner?
o   Do you relish and enjoy the trophy role?
o   Are you ashamed of it and feel guilty for having trophy pictures and behaviors?

How you answer these questions is important because your trophy is important to you. To some degree, a trophy is an extension of you and your quality, status, and importance as a person. Or at least that's the way some of the world operates.

For instance, why does a man typically want a beautiful woman? Well, the answer to that probably has more to do with the woman as a trophy rather than the woman as a mate or effective lover. When a man goes out in public and is with a beautiful woman, he sends a definite message in our society. The message is "I have earned this." "I'm valuable."

Truly, it is when one falls in love that the partner becomes beautiful. NOT before!

The Value of Trophies

Trophies support, reflect and even exaggerate our own importance. When that trophy is our mate or partner, things certainly get confusing. "Could this be a healthy or a good thing", you may well ask. And my answer would be, "Yes to both, if you understand that the trophy is NOT an extension of yourself, but a possible source of pride for yourself, and joy and celebration for others"

So let's break free of old ideas and limitations, and honestly examine the value of some spirited sharing of ourselves, and others.

A Trophy Story

About twelve years ago when I lived on my boat in South Beach, Miami, Trish, my former wife, would come over and visit. Once in a while we would start up the engine, put the sails up and sail up the Intercoastal Waterway. From Miami we would motor towards Fort Lauderdale and then turn back. One morning when we did this, Trish's cute Brazilian female friend joined us.

> *You don't marry someone you can live with;*
> *you marry the person who you cannot live without.*
>
> *—Author unknown*

We were underway for about 45 minutes when I veered to starboard toward the shore. We saw a dock on which stood an older man with a fishing rod. He's just minding his own business.

"David, do you mind if I do something?" Trish yells.

"Do whatever you want." I didn't mind.

Trish proceeded to take off her bikini top.

Next her friend also took hers off. I witnessed two beautiful Brazilian topless women on the bow of my sailboat.

> *Many people will walk in*
> *and out of your life,*
> *but only true friends will leave*
> *footprints in your heart.*
>
> —Author unknown

Trish yells, "Go closer to the fisherman."

We were only thirty yards from the dock, and he looked up. He couldn't believe what he saw. He literally almost fell in the water. Trish and her friend started waving, and of course, he returned the greeting. He had such a wonderful, excited, enthusiastic, childish grin on his face from ear to ear. As the women waved and shook their butts, he mimicked them in laughter and joy. As we passed, he said, "Thank you. Thank you. Now I have something to tell my grandchildren." (And tell his wife, after they read this book!).

Trish and her girlfriend were full of pride and good feeling, as if they truly gave this stranger a gift of spirit and excitement. I felt pride because they were kind of an extension of my manhood and value. It was a wonderful trophy experience, which Trish and I still consider a truly fond memory.

And Why Not?

What is wrong with feeling pride when others see your partner as a real plus? Is it demeaning or detrimental?

I don't believe it is demeaning when viewed in the light of having an opportunity for joy and giving. If I go out with Keaw, sometimes I ask her to put on an extra sexy dress to reveal her beautiful figure. For example, the other day we decided to play pool, and I literally went into that pool hall with Keaw as if I'd caught the largest, sleekest shark around.

Not only was she my catch, but my catch wanted me to be her honored fisherman. She's with me because she sees value in me also. What a joyous expression of mutual value that we shared through that perspective. Can you get that????

About the Afterglow

Can you have good sex and have an intellectual conversation at the same time? I think not! The heart, body and intellect co-exist, but sometimes utilization of one overshadows the other, or at least distracts one's attention sufficiently to be diminishing.

Save the intellectual discourse for later. Enjoy the moment, and share basic feelings, preferably using one syllable words like "wow," "gee," "ooooh," and "yum yum." There's nothing shallow about fully enjoying your partner physically. And, by all means, turn OFF the TV and Cell Phones! No texting before, during, or after, please! Keep your eyes on the road (or whatever!!!).

There's also nothing shallow about enjoying your partner intellectually; or for a period of time, not engaging in tactile stimulation or sex. Understanding that these are different ways of connecting is vital.

We've discussed the true intimacy of sharing pure feelings with your partner—just sitting down sometimes, without over-verbalizing or expressing strong emotion in front of another person. We trust each other to not fix, correct, modify, diminish, distract, or extract. To be there with no other agenda except presence says "I'm here with you." That's enough.

A Blonde Game of Intelligence
(Sorry about that you sensitive souls!)

There was a blonde who found herself sitting next to a lawyer on an airplane. The lawyer just kept bugging the blonde wanting her to play a game of intelligence. Finally, the lawyer offered her 10 to 1 odds, and said every time the blonde could not answer one of his questions, she owed him $5, but every time he could not answer hers, he'd give her $50.00. The lawyer figured he could not lose, and the blonde reluctantly accepted.
The lawyer first asked,
"What is the distance between the Earth and the nearest star?"
Without saying a word the blonde handed him $5. Then the blonde asked,
"What goes up a hill with 3 legs and comes back down the hill with 4 legs?"
Well, the lawyer looked puzzled. He took several hours, looking up everything he could on his laptop and even placing numerous air-to-ground phone calls trying to find the answer.
Finally, angry and frustrated, he gave up and paid the blonde $50.00. The blonde put the $50 into her purse without comment, but the lawyer insisted,
"What is the answer to your question?"
Without saying a word, the blonde handed him $5.

Intimacy Principles

Up to this point, we've covered topics that keep us from intimacy—like media scripts for love, our limiting beliefs, closed ideas, ego games or lack of self-worth and comfort with our emotions. Even untimely utilization of cell phones!

We've learned never to surrender our values, strengths and beliefs in a relationship, because we'll feel captured and suffocate in that prison. We've reviewed intimacy from differing perspectives of honesty, sexuality, emotionality, authenticity and presence. Next, I'll summarize principles of intimacy that help us stay focused on the true goals of our partnership

1—Deal with Issues Today

The spirit in most relationships needs rejuvenation. It's a dynamic process, of continuous movement, because it is of the mind and heart. As soon as we've reached a state of comfort or "bliss," the flow of life changes again. You have to keep the relationship fluid so it does not become stale. So deal with issues today as they happen.

One of the errors that people often make in a relationship is to judge (or even terminate) the relationship based on negative feelings. At any particular moment in time and space, your intimate experiences might not be where you want them to be. So your feelings are not what you desire. Your mood is somewhat glum. Your needs seem to be overwhelming and your passions seem to be diminished. "Run away, do something." Yipes!

This reaction is always counterproductive as is ignoring your feelings.

"Deal" with your feelings today. Feelings, moods, needs and passions continuously change. Relationships are bound by commitment. There always needs to be "due process" between feelings and reaction, especially in a relationship.

2—Consider Other Options

Focus on what's really happening inside.

Clients used to complain about being confused and I'd say "That's great; we're making some terrific progress here." Confusion is a breeding ground for change and growth. So if you are really filled with life experience and have learned how to deal with things effectively without throwing things away needlessly, causing unnecessarily suffering for yourself and others, then that's okay. Until you get to that point, however, don't get stuck in any kind of strong ideas because it just stops the flow and the learning.

Usually we try to avoid our confusion and the discomfort of our own reality. We give it a name, label, put it in a place, medicate it, explain it, or shift it.

Don't start blocking it! Let it flow a little bit longer. Feel all of your emotions richly. The whole name of this game is to feel it, put it in perspective and honor it. Dance with it, play with it, celebrate it, all that.

3—Honor Silence, but Avoid Repression

Let's jump right to the next principle. Controlled silence is forbidden. Aggressive silence is one of the deadliest and effective controlling tools that people use in conversation and controversy. Not that silence innately is bad, but when used inappropriately, it can be deadly. It's punishing, controlling, suffocating and aggressive.

In case you couldn't tell in my wording, silence intending to relay a message of disdain or anger is unacceptable. So if an interchange of words is necessary to complete a resolution of conflict, silence becomes a violation of the agreement if one party stops interchanging words. Keep talking or at least start kissing and hugging—but never shut down.

4—Don't Retreat

Along with silence, may I suggest that you stay physically present? Don't walk out on your partner as it violates one person's rights and privilege to communicate. If you leave the scene in order to avoid further conflict, you also avoid any resolution of the conflict. So, unless you cannot trust yourself to not react violently, you need to stay where you are. That's pretty simple.

Another rule that is worth mentioning again: <u>No</u> physical violence is acceptable during conflict or confrontation. There is no exception to this.

5—Don't Bring It to Bed

There should never be a fight, severe disagreement or continued disharmony in bed or even in the bedroom. I've observed that this will permanently diminish your ability to be comfortable and trust the space and the safety of that particular location.

That negative experience is imprinted in us emotionally and spiritually, and it can never be erased. If you need to talk through a disagreement, get out of the bedroom and do it somewhere else. It's a violation of space and purpose.

Principles of Relationship Maintenance

Now that we've reflected on some of the basic principles of a strong intimate relationship, let's consider what it takes to maintain that relationship, and allow it to grow!

1—Change Patterns of Physical Interaction Often

I mentioned in the beginning of the book that we have the ability to tune out certain repetitive behaviors. We become desensitized as part of our survival and functioning mechanism.

For example, when we take a certain route driving in the car repeatedly, especially at the same time of day, it is often a common experience that we don't even realize that we've driven the route. Our mind goes blank; we think about something else, and before we know it, we're home.

Well, unfortunately the same pattern happens when you're touching and interacting physically with another person. If the pattern is so limited and established as to be repeated every time, a desensitization of that experience occurs; it becomes less and less poignant and conscious.

In order to maintain mindfulness and consciousness in this physical interaction, it's very important to change the type, sequence, and style of interaction that we have. This would hold the interest of the body and the mind!

Changing positions makes it more interesting and engaging and spirited during touching, foreplay, play, and after-play. Touch people mindfully in places that they haven't been touched before. If you come into the kitchen in the morning and your habit is to kiss your spouse or not even to touch, why not touch her cheek? Why not caress his shoulder? Why not pinch each other in the butt? I go for the most delicious spots. Have fun with it. You know, do something different and experiment. Have some courage as well as common sense: before you goose them while you're walking down Main Street, you might say, "Honey, is it okay if I goose you here?"

2—*NOT from the Chandelier Tonight, Dear*

Or in the bedroom, "Honey, I'd like to maybe experience a different part of your body that I haven't even explored yet, something sensual and delightful."

To stay open-minded and flexible, change your habits: put your shoe on the other foot for the first time, get out of bed differently, sing a song, and play with each other's feet. Better yet, follow my example: In the middle of a walk, I might sweep my wife off her feet and kiss her passionately. She feels so special. I feel for that moment that we have obliterated the universe and we only have each other. We are so focused and so connected to each other. And public displays of affection are wonderful!

You and even the kids will remember these spontaneous moments as they free up everyone's tight butts.

Here's Joan's story:

"I've got to tell you, David, my parents were so straight. My mother wouldn't even allow herself to be slapped on the butt or touched much in front of us six kids. One night mother and we kids were waiting for my dad to come home for dinner, and he was way late. His company was hosting a small convention in town and mom probably expected that he come home a little tipsy. When his car pulled up in the driveway, we kids went to the window to watch what happened. He stumbled out of the car, grinning and singing. Immediately, all six of us started giggling. He was such fun as he hugged us all when he came in the door. We followed him to the kitchen, and I don't know where he got the African Violets but he had a handful. He marched up to mother, slapped her behind and kissed her in front of all of us. We kids clasped and cheered. Mother blushed and started stammering. Yet all of us remember the occasion and still talk about it at family reunions." Bravo, Joan!

Of course, It is ALWAYS better to "DO IT SOBER". But some passion is better than none!

3—Embrace Fantasy

The shiny badge of a trusting and committed relationship allows respect for expression of any feelings of insecurity, inadequacy and uncertainty. It's a further reflection of quality when partners can go beyond that and share ideas and fantasies, that if played out would be inappropriate; but as an idea and concept might be inspiring or provocative.

Remember that just because someone has a fantasy, it doesn't make him/her a bad, evil or immoral person. As human beings with standards and moral restraint we can and do often differentiate thought from behavior. But don't try that drunk.

4—Work at Being Wrong

To celebrate differences, work at being wrong. I've mentioned this before and it sounds like a paradox. Who would want to work at being wrong? Most people who embark on relationships focus on the similarities and trying to be right jointly.

The mind is always trying to "connect the dots", truly believing that outcome and experience itself can be managed and controlled be thorough investigation and projection. Sorry, kids, this is a mighty tempting concept, but just not true. Things happen the way they happen. And if there appears to be a certain definitive alignment between cause and effect, it is at best fleeting, and non-sequitur.

A case in point: On a certain dating website, I read that "my partner should act this way, have certain personality traits, be self-confident, attractive, intelligent, keep fit, be energetic, like outdoor activities, ad nauseum." All these different requisites, if manifested and complied with, are supposed to guarantee longevity and permanence (where these is none!). More likely, what happens eventually is that there will be so much similarity between each partner that they will get bored with each other quite quickly. Then have a good excuse to dump him or her to seek excitement and stimulation.

The elements that create the dynamics of passion and interest within a relationship are not the commonalities; they are, in fact, the differences.

Passion as we might translate it in the way of sexuality is between yin and yang, male and female. There's an energy that's created when the two are brought close together, but there's no surrender of gender or one's own true nature in the process.

In other words, when we merge, the male doesn't become more female and the female doesn't become more male. That spiritual principle of difference should be applied throughout the relationship. To go further, there are two concepts here:

o   work at being wrong,
o   being wrong is to work at not feeling compelled or controlled into being right

5—Beware of Repression Wearing the Clothes of Compromise

A caveat: Remember that creating honesty within an established relationship is a process. Beware of saying "Okay, the rules are new and now I'm going to tell you how I really feel . . ." This could literally destroy the relationship.

Every compromise to honesty, even small, is significant and if allowed to grow and fester, will cause the relationship to be less meaningful and more deceptive.

I have found that certain relationships develop such a degree of shallowness and mutual deception, that to suddenly introduce honesty and genuineness in the relationship might very well destroy it. As this process of introducing a new truth or honesty is presented to your partner, there will likely be discomfort and the feeling of abandonment and even disloyalty. However, know that you've taken another step up the ladder of intimacy.

The relationship is just not prepared, and the individuals in it are not yet strong enough to handle it. But this CAN change.

6—Take Baby Steps in Honesty

So, what do you do if you want to start being honest?

The best way that I've found is to start with someone who is not so threatened by that honesty; perhaps you can practice with a friend, relative, but <u>do not</u> choose someone who may become a substitute, present or potential lover. You know the dialogue from THAT movie.. "my wife/ husband just does not understand me. But you do! So let's go to bed!!!!".

Men and women go to potential lovers, and they start sharing their innermost feelings, dreams, aspirations and truths. They present to the lover what they cannot tell their partner. That is a lie because they could. They've just chosen not to.

Please be selective. I have found that if you're in a relationship that has grown cold and shallow, one of the ways to correct that is by starting to experiment with truth in the relationship; but tread carefully.

7—Make Love, Even When Everything's Fine

Continue to make love even through periods of stress and discomfort. This is a difficult one because it appears to be hypocritical. Again it poses the question of whether you should make love to your partner even though you're not fully inspired and you're not feeling tremendously romantic and amorous at that particular moment. The answer to the question is YES. Do so with the understanding that you won't fake it. It's okay to make love without inspiration.

About a month ago, Keaw and I were having late nights with our young daughter. Keaw and I both felt stressed, and of course, uncomfortable and exhausted. So we got into bed and thought, "Oh this is good, Jennifer is sleeping, let's make love." About ten minutes later, I'm enjoying it and I hear Keaw snoring. This may be a most embarrassing moment, yet one of the most real and important! I spanked her lovingly in the morning!

No love-making points for me from that experience! But absolutely an increase in trust and true intimacy in our relationship!

Faith is the bird that sings whilst the dawn is still dark.

—Rabindranath Tagore

Afterglow—Points to Remember

- Valuing yourself and your assets is an important principle of intimacy.
- The elements that create the dynamics of passion and interest within a relationship are not the commonalities; they are, in fact, the differences, and even disagreements.

I Wonder if
I put enough change
in the parking meter?
I wonder
what our
kids will
look like?

Chapter 11

Continuing our Daily Growth

The value of being wrong, and admitting it!!!

Unknowing—The Primary Relationship

In *The Cloud of Unknowing,* the author, a Catholic mystic, explains that the only way we truly come closer to our deepest truths is by "unknowing." In other words, the way to be truly authentic in our intimacy is to come to relationships with a clear mind. Let all previous experience and supposed knowledge slip away.

In this case, clueless is good. Keaw and Jennifer can attest to the fact that I'm pretty good at that!

Here is what unknowing really means:

- Letting go of concepts and information
- Having no expectations.
- Making no assumptions.
- Being free of intrusive thoughts
- Having an empty mind (Works for me. Ask Keaw, or JJ!)

Imagine that your two hands lift your head off your shoulders, turn it upside down over a trash can, and shake all the contents of your head into the trash. When you return your head to your shoulders, there's an amazing rush of unknowing, a sense of emptiness and calm.

> *Empty your mind; be formless, shapeless—like water.*
> *Now you put water into a cup, it becomes the cup,*
> *you put water into a bottle,*
> *it becomes the bottle, you put it in a teapot, and it becomes the teapot.*
> *Now water can flow or it can crash. Be water, my friend.*
>
> —Bruce Lee

You clear your mind and are open to all potential and possibilities in yourself and in your intimate relationships. Unknowing is an absolute foundation for continuing to take a personal inventory and correcting responses as you continue daily growth.

During this openness, intimacy becomes an experience that you breathe and walk, not an idea in your mind. This is primal relationship—when you allow pure experience to enter and forget about the old ways, the past, the pictures and all the rest.

Simply enjoying a flower is an example of an unknowing experience. You're not translating the flower's color into a word. You're not interpreting the aroma according to any past experience. You're not comparing the size of the flower to another one. You're not even concerned about where the flower came from. The word *flower* becomes meaningless; it's just a total experience.

I offer you guidelines for sustaining your intimacy, with a few reminders for never surrendering selfhood.

Relationships and Elephants

Intimate relationships, like the flower, can be total experiences if you enter and maintain the relationship out of choice rather than belief or need. Relationships based on choice are fluid with an inherent sense of lightness and room to breathe. They are delightful rather than demanding and restraining.

Choosing a relationship is a matter of perspective, like the difference between viewing the back end or the front end of an elephant. If you look from the back end, all you see is a big butt, and nothing really worthwhile (unless you're a hungry fly!)..

If you look at the front of the creature, you see a beautiful trunk and friendly eyeballs smiling at you. Same animal, different perspective.

The *Rules* of Intimacy

Yep, I know! You think I've totally lost it here. We've been discussing flexibility, malleability, diversity, and spiritual anarchy, and now we're already citing rules.

Well, I have found that the more diverse and open-minded you are willing to be, the more you need to establish and apply a basic framework to your decisions, your behaviors, your perspectives, and your life. This is especially true when you are engaged in the lifelong challenge and pleasure of a truly intimate, committed relationship.

So, pilgrims, stay with me on this. Understand that these are spiritual principles, not behavioral. Your attitude and intent are vital. And there, always seek integrity!

Rule #1
No Comparisons

So if you're going to live with an elephant, I always recommend that you stay in front of the elephant rather behind. You cannot compare one end to the other any more than you can compare your relationship to those seen on television or to another's idea of how it is supposed to be.

Stop comparing your relationship to others, or to those presented in the media. There is *no* relevancy!

In a relationship, stay on the lighter, brighter, smiling side. Choose the perspective of freedom rather than burden. That way you get intimacy without surrender because you're voluntarily engaging without saying, "I surrender. I'm giving something up. My relationship doesn't look as great as my neighbor's."

> *Adam and Eve had an ideal marriage. He didn't have to hear about all the men she could have married, and she didn't have to hear about the way his mother cooked.*

Here is a simplified view of how to choose relationships for intimacy:

The Captured Viewpoint: "I'm not autonomous in my life. I'm not really independent. I can't be a free spirit and a committed partner too.

The Freedom Viewpoint: "Yes, I will involve and commit myself to this true, close, caring, and honest relationship. All the time I know that I'm still a free spirit. I'm still independent. I haven't merged my spirit into another human being although I share my spirit. I don't give up my freedom; I share my freedom. I don't give up my will, I share my will."

You *do* see the big difference between the front and back of the elephant, right? If you approach a relationship by choice and are willing to work to support it, the relationship can be full of life. You aren't comparing your relationship to any others. Rather, you're continuing to grow and living in the truest style of your life. Be light-hearted in all aspects of the relationship. And check out the elephant's butt periodically!

Rule #2
Continue to Review and Correct

Good relationships, by nature, are not oppressive or limiting. If at any time you feel that you are being captured or your autonomy is compromised, be willing to share this with your partner. Be prepared for defense and some contention, but always get back to expressing the feelings, not justifying them!

If your relationship becomes oppressive or limiting, follow these two simple steps.

Step One: Review your part in the relationship.

Remember—it's always "let it begin with me!" When you're pointing the finger at someone else, you're avoiding responsibility.

Of course, your partner's actions are very likely "eliciting" or justifying feelings (some of which you just don't like), but they are not "causing" the feelings. Your feelings are yours and yours alone.

Understand and apply this concept, and you will be amazed at how many apparent conflicts and battles are resolved, diffused, or totally eliminated.

And then you're left with enjoying the main benefit of all relationships, to be totally who and what you are, and to be loved for (and in spite) of it!

Step Two: Answer these questions and then make the correction

o   How are you approaching it?
o   What are your expectations or demands?
o   Are these demands realistic, or merely self-serving?
o   What are the "stories" or emotional memories that you are replaying in your head that are resulting in a dead-end for you and your partner?
o   How much energy are you expending in defending and/or justifying your disappointment, upset, anger or whatever feeling? If it's more than a few moments, back up and re-group soldier! The battlefield itself is YOU!

Intimacy's Reflection

How does a good relationship feel and look? It feels and looks like your partner is a cheerleader. Not only is your partner your personal enthusiast, but also a supporter who is willing to encourage you in whatever decision you make, even if that decision is contrary to the one that s/he would make in the same circumstance.

Why? Because your life journey is your own; you walk it as an individual in any relationship. This fact of life cannot and should not be changed.

Unimportant, and even important, decisions should be examined, discussed, debated, and even argued about (if that's your cup of tea). But the result and final decision, if it is a personal compromise or violation, is NOT justified, or justifiable.

> *When the daylight's gone and you're on your own*
> *And you need a friend just to be around*
> *I will comfort you; I will take your hand*
> *And I'll pull you through, I will understand.*
>
> *At Your Side* by The Cars

The concept that you're locked arm-in-arm, shoulder-to-shoulder, and joined hip-to-hip, is wrong. If you think intimacy is an experience of being so totally together and with constant mutual agreement and shared focus, then your view is defective. It even goes further than defective; that concept is actually destructive. So, honestly, does this sound like you?

Joined at the Hip Intimacy Quiz

So you're definitely on a relationship pink cloud, a wonderful experience, without a doubt! But take this test (true/false) and see how absorbed in these myths you truly are:

I always sing, "Together, together, forever, forever . . ."
I truly believe the guy who wrote the book called *Soul Mates*. I just have to figure out how to replicate that.
I believe my intimate partner and I must do everything together.
I believe my partner is my twin flame, and we are cosmically destined to burn brightly for eternity.
I think that my wonderful intimate and I should think alike, never disagree and be nice to each other all the time.

If you answered true to even one of the above statements, you are indeed captured.

What if that wonderful merging experience with your intimate partner actually becomes a stifling and suffocating experience? What if you suddenly wake up with some spiritual enlightenment or personal acknowledgement which causes you to conclude: "Oh my god, I'm carrying this whole relationship! I've gone from point A to point B, and now I have grown in wisdom while the other half hasn't? What do I do?"

What is the usual next step of the not-intimates? Lift finger, point at partner and say, "You made me do it. You insisted that I be this. You insisted that I dress this way. You insisted that I look this way. It's your entire fault. So there!" Oh my! Begging to be captured—and done, baby!

Rule #3
You Are Responsible

When you shift your perception from the front of the elephant to the back end, you are responsible for the shift, not your partner. You've personally changed positions and now must own it.

For whatever reasons, we've surrendered parts of ourselves that should never have been surrendered. This was out of fear of rejection, being alone, judgment, not being accepted or loved by another.

This truth is difficult to own: *Not only have I been captured, I've been the force behind the capture.* Not only have I created an enemy, I've gone to the enemy and I said to the enemy, "Take me."

You create the enemy, and then you surrender to the enemy, and then you hate the enemy. Somehow you feel that your essence or your nature is compromised, altered, modified or dissipated. Here is how you can gain perspective.

Ask and answer these questions for yourself.

- o How did this happen?
- o How did I get here?
- o How did I create this?
- o What do I tell myself about this perception?
- o How true are the facts that support this premise in real life?
- o Am I willing to change my perception or view the situation differently?

Rule #4
Have No Dishonesty (to thy own self be true)

Until you acknowledge and accept the fact that not only are you a willful participant in this process, you're probably the instigator and initiator of the whole problem. Only at that point can you start working on a solution.

If you cannot acknowledge the self-responsibility, then perhaps you've been lying to yourself as well as your partner. If you've developed a pattern of dishonesty in the relationship, then experiment with honesty with someone else first. Take the time to talk honestly with a friend, rabbi, pastor, or poodle—that is, someone you trust to hold your confidence. Sweat through getting the words out and take the risk.

Talking it through may help you see more clearly, take responsibility, and ask, "So how can I change?" The answer to the question is:

o   Know what your needs are.
o   Put them into perspective.
o   Get whatever help and support is necessary.
o   Carry on with life and become more of whom and what you truly deserve to be.

Rule #5
Continue to share honestly, even when it hurts

Being truly honest with someone you love is one of the most difficult tasks of a relationship. There are so many risks involved!

It is almost always less effort to take the easy way out: Avoid conflict. Skirt issues. Deceive by omission.

The excuse people typically use to justify this damaging behavior saying they are just sparing the feelings of the other person. I've even heard partners justify secret love affairs, relationships, and other violations of their relationship standard by claiming that they are so concerned about hurting the other person with the truth, that lies are better!

I have only one thing to say about this approach, and attitude: Poppycock!

> *A wife, one evening, drew her husband's attention to the couple next door and said, "Do you see that couple?*
> *How devoted they are? He kisses her every time they meet.*
> *Why don't you do that?"*
> *"I would love to," replied the husband,*
> *"but I don't know her well enough."*

Drain the Swamp

Often my friends report to me their difficulties in being motivated to change.

- They are willing.
- They can identify the problem.
- They are aware of solutions.
- Then taking the first step to change is like running into a glass wall. Bang!

Perhaps it helps to remind ourselves that when we are up to our asses in alligators, our primary purpose is to drain the swamp. When life becomes sufficiently uncomfortable or painful, we find adequate motivation to change, or even we get MORE spiritual, and just DO IT! Let's face this ultimate fact about ourselves: When drowning, we do swim harder and find the necessary energy to shift our speed and responses. Sound like anyone you know?

> *How do some men define marriage?*
> *"An expensive way to get laundry done for free." (So crass!)*

The Intimacy Paradox

One reason people find change difficult is the paradox of intimacy itself: You want to be totally free and independent in the relationship.

Yet, your belief that you have to surrender clashes with the desire for freedom. At the same time, you need to commit and be responsible for true intimacy. Let me reiterate the underlying truths of the intimacy paradox:

- o **Surrender no part of yourself.** What you value is the foundation for intimate relationships; so sorting through and defining your values is critical. I suggest that you define what you need to defend as well as protect within a relationship. You are not willing to give up these attributes. Stand firm.
- o **Be aware.** Remind yourself that bumping into the glass wall is a wake-up call to identify the problems and make corrections so growth continues.
- o **Come with unknowing:** When you review and clear your expectations, you find solutions in the empty spaces between busy thoughts. The point is to sort through who you are, what you are, and what makes you feel right about yourself. If the relationship that you're in or contemplating being in, requires surrender of any of those core elements of your person, then the relationship needs to be restructured.

On their 40th wedding anniversary and during the banquet celebrating it, Tom was asked to give his friends a brief account of the benefits of a marriage of such long duration.

"Tell us Tom, just what is it you have learned from all those wonderful years with your wife?"

Tom responds, "Well, I've learned that marriage is the best teacher of all. It teaches you loyalty, forbearance, meekness, self-restraint, forgiveness—and a great many other qualities you wouldn't have needed if you'd stayed single."

Rule #6
Stop Talking, and Start (fill in the blank)

How do we make intimacy work? How do we arrive at willingness to change? When you face such overwhelmingly significant questions of how to make it work and you need those answers, then stop talking. When you think that you have to work hard at getting some semblance of continuity and consistency in the relationship, then, be quiet at that point.

When all your instincts are screaming, "You've got to restructure. This is important. Talk now. Find the time. Hurry up, your life is waiting. We have demands and disappointments, blah blah . . ."

Stop talking and start touching.

This is critical. When you're aware that there's a problem and you're in concert, both desiring the resolve, then stop the dialogue and be with each other for a while. Don't come up with answers or solutions at that point. STOP!

I believe that people make a grave error at this crucial point in their partnership journey when they want to redevelop a whole paradigm about how their relationship should look and feel.

Don't go cognitive. Get back in touch!

Over analyzing situations and relationship dynamics is an interesting distraction, but is not effective in resolving problems, or making the relationship stronger and more honest.

If and when you find yourself bantering words and concepts back and forth, without any apparent progress, *stop*!

It's time to get back to basics. A gentle touch, caring look, sensuous massage, a knowing smile, or a familiar song sung in harmony without benefit of a common key. Now that's intimacy!

> *Men who want their marriages to succeed should just do what their wives suggest.*
> *Psychologist John Gottman says that advice to engage in "active listening" and other interactive ways to resolve differences may be on the wrong track. Gottman's team followed 130 newlyweds for six years, tracking how they handled disagreement.*
> *Many tried the "active listening" model, which calls for each person to re-phrase what the other has said. They found the people who stayed together rarely used such listening techniques.*
> *The marriages that seemed to work had one thing in common— the husband was willing to be influenced by his wife. One of the participants, Gomer Ludlow, said, "To keep her happy, and for more chances for me to get laid, I just let her think she's getting her way and then do it my way."*
>
> —John Gottman, *The Relationship Cure*

Rule #7
Continue to Make Love, No Matter What!

Through periods of stress and discomfort, what is more comforting than making love? Whether you explore in delicate touching and deep arousal or zap the tension with mutual, delightful groans of passion, you are continuing to communicate and touch (sorry for the pun) each other. You still risk sharing and have not turned away. Touch requires no words, yet also invites openness.

This approach requires the greatest of courage, trust and commitment. What you value is the foundation for intimate relationships; so sorting through and defining your values is critical.

> *At the end of what is called the "sexual life" the only love that has lasted is the love which has everything, every failure and every betrayal, which has accepted even the sad fact that in the end there is no desire so deep as the simple desire for companionship.*
>
> —Graham Greene

Afterglow—Points to Remember

- o "Unknowing" is an absolute foundation for continuing to take a personal inventory and correcting responses as you stretch and grow.
- o Relationships based on choices (NOT beliefs) are fluid with an inherent sense of lightness and room to breathe.
- o By nature and right understanding, good relationships are not oppressive, but freeing.
- o Always review your part in any relationship and take responsibility for making those changes that need to be made. Always to make it BETTER!
- o Surrender no part of yourself. Value your character traits.
- o Stop talking and start loving.

I Think it's time we took this relationship to the next level.

Chapter 12

Never Standing Still in a Relationship

Continuing growth in all relationships.

Personal Growth Sustains Intimacy

Perhaps you noticed in the last chapter that my emphasis for finding true intimacy is on being true to yourself and exploring the unknown. You know that the ebb and flow of life is forever changing and challenging us to continue learning adapting and hopefully flowing. Change often seems to create a tension from which some of us shy away, especially if we feel naïve in addressing tense conversations, as I once was. You've got to be yourself—and you are the only one who can speak for you. Understand, engage and embrace the tension. To your own self be true to avoid the capture-surrender games.

A judge was interviewing a woman regarding her pending divorce,
"What are the grounds for your divorce?"
She replied, "About four acres and a nice little home in the middle
of the property."
"I mean," he continued, "What are your relations like?"
"I have an aunt and uncle living here in town, and so do my
husband's parents."
He said, "Do you have a real grudge?"
"No," she replied, "We have a two-car carport and have never really
needed one."

> *"Please," he tried again, "is there any infidelity in your marriage?"*
> *"Yes, both my son and daughter have stereo sets. We don't necessarily like the music, but the answer to your question is 'yes'."*
> *"Ma'am, does your husband ever beat you up?"*
> *"Yes," she responded, "most days he gets up earlier than I do."*
> *Finally, in frustration, the judge asked, "Lady, why do you want a divorce?"*
> *"Oh, I don't want a divorce," she replied. "I never wanted a divorce. It's my husband.*
> *For some reason he says he can't communicate with me."*

Tension is the CORE of Passion

I think this heading really needs expansion because so few people honor tension or deal with it well in relationships. So listen up and take my words to heart. My advice will create endless hours of peaceful and fulfilling passion for you!

In our intimate relationships, each of us takes responsibility for developing and growing our own "self-hood", or what we like to imagine ourselves to be. Instead of working at being the same as your partner, the process is now different. And you are challenged to accept and *honor* the differences.

People often shy away from confrontation or avoid the friction created by dynamics of emotions. In so doing a vital energy is eliminated in the relationship.

Rule #8
Celebrate Differences

o   Didn't we join in order to be more like each other?
o   Didn't we want to melt into each other's lives?

Absolutely not! We're not joined at any juncture of the body, mind, or spirit. We are sharing our lives, but not our perceived selves. Inherent in this enlightened pairing is friction.

There is tension whenever there are differences of focus, perception, values, or even moods and feelings. You have been lied to about how needs and uniqueness are supposed to diminish in relationships. If they do, passion itself dies!

Embrace tension. Accept friction. That's the only choice for real intimacy, otherwise you follow the standard rules and find yourself captured—roped and hog tied.

Let the rebel in you practice being wrong now and then. Have some fun! The more you play at being wrong, being different, walking backwards, breaking a few rules, the more you desensitize yourself. Play becomes more important than being right and thinking you know the rules of how relationships look, smell, act, and talk. Or even believing that the rules are worth knowing, never mind following!

Silly Rules:

1. *The Female always makes THE RULES.*
2. *THE RULES are subject to change without notice.*
3. *No Male can possible know all THE RULES.*
4. *If the Female suspects the Male knows all THE RULES, she must immediately change some of THE RULES.*
5. *The Female is never wrong.*
6. *If it appears the Female is wrong, it is because of a flagrant misunderstanding caused by something the Male did or said wrong.*
7. *If Rule #6 applies, the Male must apologize immediately for causing the misunderstanding.*
8. *The Female can change her mind at any time.*
9. *The Male must never change his mind without the express, written consent of the Female.*
10. *The Female has every right to be angry or upset at any time and blame it on the partner, or a biological function.*

> 11. *The Male must remain calm at all times, unless the Female wants, expects, or demands him to be angry or upset.*
> 12. *The Female must, under no circumstances, let the Male know whether she wants him to be angry or upset.*
> 13. *The Male is expected to read the mind of the Female at all times.*
> 14. *At all times, what is important is what the Female meant, not what she said.*
> 15. *If the Male doesn't abide by THE RULES, it is because he can't take the heat, lacks backbone, and is a wimp.*
> 16. *If the Female has PMS, all THE RULES are null and void and the Male must cater to her every whim.*
> 17. *Any attempt to document THE RULES could result in bodily harm.*
> 18. *If the Male, at any time, believes he is right, he must refer to Silly Rule #5."*

Rule #9
Stay Empowered

When tension in a relationship is supported and honored because of your immutable commitment, it can re-ignite the passion and the joy of your relationship on a daily basis.

"Why, Edsel?" you may ask. That sounds so... Edsel Terrick! The answer is that now you are being empowered instead of being diminished in the partnership.

You are empowered in the partnership to be yourself and to celebrate YOU, not your demise or false face. Finally one person on a consistent basis will love you and care about you, even when you agree that the differences are glaring, and irresolvable (because they are merely imagined).

Use those differences for mutual empowerment. Imagine the fireworks when you embrace diversity. Imagine the possibilities when you truly touch each other from different places, not the same.

Your combined energies are a culmination of your separate personalities and perceptions. This is the point in relationships where the sum is truly greater than the parts, because the parts are whole and not diminished.

Enjoy your womanhood and enjoy your manhood fully because it is the tension of genders that brings spirit, joy and sparkling intimacy. And if you are of like gender, celebrate your differences of experience, perspective, and consciousness.

When you empower your differences, you'll find there's no reason to apologize to yourself or to each other. There is no violation, surrender, or capture.

You're reaffirming your belief and trust in another person when you approach that person as yourself. When you feel the need to give that up, then you're truly diminishing your respect and your reflection of trust in your partner.

Rule #10
Tell the Truth with Kindness

If in doubt, take the risk and speak your truth, even if it means you believe that you might hurt the other person.

People in relationships get off track if truth comes out as a defensive action or is distorted into a justification or a reason. Be aware that when you get into a defensive position, sometimes you distort your perception. That doesn't necessarily reflect your truth.

However, if you express your perceived truth in a manner that acknowledges and is sensitive to the other person's reaction, you are being honest and not offensive. Never purposely elicit a hostile or defensive response. Short of that, all truth is acceptable. Remember, it is all perspective or opinion anyway! The mind continuously creates ideas that it puts in its "truth" bin.

How is this different from Rule #5? Well, the main principle here is to not only shore your "truth", but to express it with love and sensitivity. Not with a heavy dose of sugar-coating!

Ah, you wise wabbits ask "Edsel, exactly what IS truth? And don't get all Edsel Terrick with us!"

OK. Truth is what someone honestly believes and feels inside, being expressed completely to the other person without blame, hostility, or aggression. With the realization that it is a movement, NOT a state.

Share All

This includes interesting fantasies (forget the dull ones.), ideas, daydreams, visions, feelings of frustration and all of the imaginings, reactions, dreams and unfounded assumptions that go on inside of you whilst you are chasing the rabbit. The expectation in expressing these "truths" to our partner is not to motivate change either in the other person or ourselves, but to simply acknowledge what seems to be so, right now. Even if misperceived or misinterpreted

Truth-telling is an experience of sharing that supports intimacy, even in the darkest times of shared and grieving. When you allow this process to happen, when you develop this degree of trust and comfort with another person, you have cause to celebrate.

> *He valued emotion—not for itself,*
> *but because it is the only final path to intimacy.*
>
> —Edward Morgan Forster

You get these positive benefits when you can tell your partner the your truth:

o   You are being true to your character and/or present beliefs.
o   You are taking a risk.
o   You are expressing yourself without feeling that you are violating yourself or the other person.
o   You can be vulnerable (and WRONG!) in your truth. This is tremendously critical to a relationship.

This thing called "truth" is one of the foundation stones of intimacy. To be able to talk about what's inside you, and be heard, even if it doesn't conform to the other person's ideas or expectations, validates mutual trust and commitment. Expressing your truth and having your partner be surprised, confused or even challenged, ultimately results in a higher degree of intimacy.

Truth is like a surprise package. You don't think you'll end up with a gift because the process feels painful or uncomfortable. Yet, you do! Again, we are going back to the beginning of the book and challenging the fact that what you're seeing and expecting in creating and maintaining intimate relationships are not really valid and realistic.

Feeling exposed, vulnerable and tender, even to the degree of not feeling a sense of trust in your partner; yet staying with the partner and continuing to communicate, are all indicators of wonderful relationship.

o   DO NOT stay on safe ground.
o   Risk the sharing of your fantasies
o   Trust that your intimate partner will not run away, nor will you.
o   Promise (and honor that promise) that you'll never use any intimate information for attack or anger.
o   Promise that any secrets and this communication shall always be safe.
o   Never violate the promise to protect and hold safe the information.
o   Make the promise and <u>mean it</u>, regardless of future feelings or circumstances.

These are true commitments. This spiritual and practical groundwork is critical to consistent growth in a truly intimate relationship.

> *My experience suggests that intimacy has two main components:*
> *Risk and commitment. Risk and commitment both require*
> *decisions.*
> *Our society, in accepting and fostering the values portrayed*
> *by much of the media,*
> *is engaged in the systematic destruction of its ability to*
> *recognize, nurture, and risk intimate relations."*
>
> —Victor L. Brown

The (SACRED) Rules of Engagement

Didn't think Edsel would use such a strong word as "sacred" did you? But please understand that the Rules of engagement are suggested protocols or procedures **to effectively not agree**. In other words, let me tell you how to have a fair fight and make it meaningful, productive and nurturing. And—you might even have some fun and laugh your way through the tensions.

How to Fight Without Winning or Losing . . .

- If you understand the principles of this book, then you understand that in many life arenas, the battles and fights seem to require a winner and a loser.
- In relationships, however, if there is in fact a winner and a loser, the fight has contributed to destroying the relationship rather than reinforcing it.
- Arguments between people in committed intimate relationships need to end with no clear winner and no clear loser.

There is a process and approach to not agreeing that many of us have never learned. Moreover, we've never seen the positive results of approaching disagreement in this manner.

- During a period of controversy, allow each partner an opportunity to speak completely and separately without interruption.
- Build time boundaries that allow a pause between when one person finishes speaking and the other person starts speaking. An agreed to internal "STOP!". Two people competing with each other causes unnecessary hostility and competition.
- Whoever presented the controversy has the exclusive right to contain the dialogue to the matter first presented.

Example of Application

Say I'm angry with Keaw. For the sake of our intimacy and prolonged relationship, I decide that I'm going to share my anger and frustration with her. I get her attention and say, "Keaw, let me tell you how I'm feeling—five minutes ago I was trying to get your attention while you were on the phone. I thought it was really important that I talk to you; I wanted you to pay attention to me and you totally ignored me . . ."

This is a critical juncture in a conflict (dialogue); Keaw has two choices at that point....

1. She listens actively so she understands what is being said and why. The communication is not to condemn, correct or place blame. It is merely to express.

2. Keaw defends and justifies her actions. Then she moves on to recalling and verbalizing past hurt feelings and perceived violations in order to put this situation in another perspective. In other words, the message is, "Hey, I might have done something wrong, but you have done dozens of things wrong. So shut up, buster, or I'll clobber you."

Unfortunately most people make the second choice, responding to a complaint with another complaint out of defense or fear or even anger.

Never, ever, ever do that! That's not allowed! TIME OUT KIDS!

It's natural that it happens because once my anger is expressed, then Keaw may want to also express hers. However, it dilutes and distracts the whole point of the dialogue in the conflict. So instead of one issue, now we've got two or MORE, because of stored emotional memories).

A couple was having a discussion about family finances. Finally the husband exploded, 'If it weren't for my money, the house wouldn't be here!' The wife replied, 'My dear, if it weren't for your money, I wouldn't be here.'

More Rules?

Okay, mea culpa. I am presenting you with some more rules. These, like the others, are vital for success, or at least unlikeliest of heartbreaking failure.

We call these the "rules of engagement." Suffice to say, if more people followed these rules, more relationships would blossom from mutual discovery and appreciation, to marriage, to living (happily) ever after!

Consider this "Bliss for Dummies"!

First Rule of Engagement

Whoever brought up the issue has the right to continue until it's resolved or no longer has much energy.

Second Rule of Engagement

Acknowledge the issue and respect that any secondary complaint must wait until the first issue is complete. This truly is vitally important!

If your partner makes a mean statement, avoid responding by saying *I wouldn't say that to you, why should you say it to me? I wouldn't do that to you, why do you do it to me? I wouldn't lie to you, why do you lie to me?*

Even if the comparison were true, it's not valid during the exchange, and labeled controversy. Your demand is that your partner be exactly like you are, and he or she is not. So, give it up!

Third Rule of Engagement

Avoid comparisons of behavior or standards during an engagement or a conflict.

As already mentioned, accept the fact that we all work with different priorities and have different standards and ways of doing things. If you have established an intimate relationship with another person, those differences are not so glaring or so pronounced that they're going to interfere with your continuing in the relationship.

So, respect the differences and stop comparing and demanding "sameness".

> *A young couple drove several miles down a country road, not saying a word.*
> *An earlier discussion had led to an argument, and neither wanted to concede their position.*
> *As they passed a barnyard of mules and pigs, the husband sarcastically asked, 'Are they relatives of yours?'*
> *'Yes,' his wife replied. 'I married into the family.'*

And "Throwing Up" or Regurgitating the Past?

"So, Edsel," you ask, "what about when my partner keeps throwing the past in my face?"

Typically, one partner mentions a certain recalled event or series of events more times than necessary. Yep, I mean your partner throws it in your face. To top it off, the event may not even be relevant to your conversation.

Recalling the event elicits anger and frustration. Understand that this is a natural function of the hungry and basically dissatisfied mind. Emotional memories shift from the past to the present (and to the future). In this realm, the mind is truly inept, ineffective, and actually CREATES disharmony and distress.

Fourth Rule of Engagement

If you can't get agreement on the event, go no further. In other words, STOP.

Example:

"You stepped on my toe in 1976, and I limped for months."
"No, I did not step on your toe. You stubbed it on the brick."
"I was there. I remember. It was my toe . . ."

"Stop. I call a truce!"

There, one of you with a sense of the rules of engagement stops. There's no reason to go any further in the process. Agree that the toe was hurt. The past is gone; that past event has no relevance to the present.

What does matter is expression of the anger and emotional intensity created from the past brought up in the present by the one with the sore toe. Incidents of the past are always about the emotions, not the event. And if you're as old as I am you might have even forgotten what happened yesterday. What a blessing!

Don't Short-Circuit the Process

Now, this next part is critical, but often misunderstood.

A lot of engagements are not defused if the partner asks forgiveness and apologizes too quickly.

Why? It produces no effective resolution in that the supposed victim has not uncovered the root feelings that he or she needed to express from this particular past event. Remember that this conversation is not about the event, but about emotions and feelings. The one who throws up the past really needs to get to the root feelings.

If you apologize and kiss the "boo-boo," the anger is still present. Love your partner enough to hear the deeper aspects of the anger. What's behind the anger?

The real emotional issue, as we know, is not anger, but it might be a feeling of betrayal, hurt feelings or insecurity. Find the source, get to those feelings first. Express it, acknowledge it.

Once there's sufficient time for expression, then the perpetrator can say, "I understand and I really do apologize, not only for the past event but I also feel sad for your present hurt feelings."

Fifth Rule of Engagement

This is important ("Edsel, you ALWAYS say that!"), Of course.

Rather than focus on the specifics of the event, or the anger around the event, listen, and have empathy and compassion (look up the meaning of that word) for, your partner's hurt feelings, disappointment, or unmet needs, justified or not.

The specific event, and what emotional charge it still contains, is *not* the problem. It should never be diagnosed as the source of the trouble.

It is the pain or distress that is experienced by the partner hearing the message that is the problem, and should be the primary focus.

So instead of engaging in a monkey dance (you *know* what that is already) about how you "didn't mean this" or "did mean that," it is much more effective to communicate that there is a true empathy and sorrow for the pain that your loved one is feeling, NOT you apparently causing it.

No retraction or excuses are necessary. They are condescending and disrespectful. Try saying (and meaning) something like, "Honey, I sincerely apologize for contributing to your hurt and pain. Please understand that was not my intention. I love you."

Sixth Rule of Engagement

If you feel disappointed, angry, violated, disrespected, ignored, abandoned, etc. as a result of a specific behavior of your partner, you have up to 24 hours to express that feeling to your partner.

Keaw and I call this our "24 hour rule." This ranks amongst the top relationship savers for us!

It's quite simple, but marvelously effective!

That's it! No longer! No stored resentments! No secret weapons to use at a later date. Either express it and go through it, or leave it. Yes, as if it never happened.

This is not as difficult as it sounds, but it does require courage and commitment.

This is a meditative practice that can be tremendously healthy to you personally. You are able to see that the mind takes the past, and makes it real in the present. Another imagining of the wabbit mind!

> *As soon as the love relationship does not lead me to me,*
> *as soon as I in a love relationship do not lead another person*
> *to himself, this love, even if it seems to be the most secure*
> *and ecstatic attachment I have ever experienced, is not true*
> *love.*
> *For real love is dedicated to continual becoming.*
>
> —Leo Buscaglia

Afterglow—Points to Remember

- In intimate relationships, each takes responsibility for developing and growing their own self-hood. Instead of the couple working at being the same, each follows their own path. The differences are honored and celebrated.
- You're reaffirming your belief and your trust in another person when you approach that other person as yourself. When you feel the need to give that up, then you're truly diminishing your respect and your reflection of trust in your partner.
- If in doubt about being honest, always take the risk and speak YOUR truth. Temper it with kindness.
- Agree to disagree.
- Respect differences in relationships and quit comparing yours to others, whether on television or in real life.
- If a partner brings up the past, the real message is about the emotion, not the event itself.
- Respect the 24-hour rule.

What a DISGUSTING display!
Lucky Bastard...
Yes, Terrible!
I wish it was me
Well I NEVER!
But I wish I did
Somebody should inform the manager!
Lucky GUY!

Chapter 13

Spreading Joy and Intimacy Throughout Your World!

*Utilizing these principles in our relationships,
and continuing our journey of love, honesty and intimacy.*

> *We come to love not by finding a perfect person,
> but by learning to see an imperfect person perfectly.*
>
> Unknown

Desiderata - Words for Life

Go placidly amid the noise and haste,
and remember what peace there may be in silence.
As far as possible without surrender
be on good terms with all persons.
Speak your truth quietly and clearly;
and listen to others,
even the dull and the ignorant;
they too have their story.

Avoid loud and aggressive persons,
they are vexations to the spirit.
If you compare yourself with others,
you may become vain and bitter;
for always there will be greater and lesser persons than yourself.
Enjoy your achievements as well as your plans.

Keep interested in your own career, however humble;
it is a real possession in the changing fortunes of time.
Exercise caution in your business affairs;
for the world is full of trickery.
But let this not blind you to what virtue there is;
many persons strive for high ideals;
and everywhere life is full of heroism.

Be yourself.
Especially, do not feign affection.
Neither be cynical about love;
for in the face of all aridity and disenchantment
it is as perennial as the grass.

Take kindly the counsel of the years,
gracefully surrendering the things of youth.
Nurture strength of spirit to shield you in sudden misfortune.
But do not distress yourself with dark imaginings.
Many fears are born of fatigue and loneliness.
Beyond a wholesome discipline,
be gentle with yourself.

You are a child of the universe,
no less than the trees and the stars;
you have a right to be here.
And whether or not it is clear to you,
no doubt the universe is unfolding as it should.

Therefore be at peace with God,
whatever you conceive Him to be,
and whatever your labors and aspirations,
in the noisy confusion of life keep peace with your soul.

With all its sham, drudgery, and broken dreams,
it is still a beautiful world.
Be cheerful.
Strive to be happy.

— Max Ehrmann, 1927

Your Relationship with The World

It is worth examining how our primary relationship with our intimate reflects the way we relate to the world-at-large, and, maybe more importantly, how we relate to "ourselves".

A cold candle cannot light itself, or even be lit by another. The lighting needs to come from within, not from without. Once the candle is lit, the flame consumes the candle, and has a reality of its own.

Does the world truly "love a lover?"

Does your comfort and joy in an intimate and truly supportive relationship reflect in other areas of your life?

Are you generally a happier person when you are feeling loved and accepted for exactly who you are?

In this book we have examined, and hopefully improved, your ability to understand the fundamental nature of intimacy and live dynamically in a fulfilling relationship. But does it stop with your partner? Absolutely not!

We are always in relationships of one form or another. Our lives move within and around relationships with friends, neighbors, co-workers, family and even strangers and iguanas. They are all of great importance.

How we approach and handle all of these relationships is vital for our integrity, and peace within ourselves and the world.

It All Begins with You

All relationships in your life begin (and sometimes end) with your attitude and perception. How do you view the world? Do you feel the world is a hostile, cold, unforgiving place full of deceit and deception? Edsel Terrickly speaking we imagine and create our own world.

Do you anticipate and expect that when you let your guard down you will be attacked and hurt? The warrior or the wounded realist in you probably responds, "You bet! The world is a harsh battleground." Or, "It's a jungle out there." Ouch!

Let's retreat and reconsider.

We've learned that it is our internal processes and perspectives that determine the quality and strength of our primary relationship. This is true of all our relationships. This truth is critical! If understood and applied, it will empower you to reshape your entire world, one relationship at a time!

Instant Karma

Again, you create your world based on your entrenched and myopic beliefs, subsequent attitude and ultimately your spiritual condition. You thought that the idea of instant karma was some pleasant philosophical concept to be considered while enjoying a drug-induced repose or listening to an old Beatles album? Nope.

The concept that for every action, there is a reaction, has merit and relevance in our world. However, you must understand that these are not always limited, or specific to, your outside behaviors. Our inner world, the real center of our universe, shapes our life also, and sometimes more profoundly than our behavior.

To try to control the world directly in any way, is both frustrating and foolish. How many times have you attempted to shift other people's attitudes and behaviors by any number of particular dances that you might do. We often deceive ourselves into believing that we can truly change another, and improve relationships, by "acting as if."

This just doesn't work. Our focus and change needs to be at a much deeper level. Though difficult, we need to allow others (even those we love and need) to be who they are and find their own paths.

Hey, nobody said this would be easy!

In this world, we often subscribe to the concept of "cause and effect". Understand please that it is the mind that creates this illusion.

The fact is that things just HAPPEN. They are not induced, created, controlled, or managed by our minds, or even our choices.

Throughout this book, we've discussed ways in which you can step back and observe the "play" on stage. Avoid feeding the reactionary energy of ghostly emotional memories from your past that are merely pain and sorrow that the mind has recorded and replaying (not necessarily for your entertainment). Now, you are learning new ways to be in relationship. Again, these include

- The need to live and let live.
- To disagree without being disagreeable.
- The art of being wrong, and how to allow others to be wrong.

The Delicate Balance

Being onstage and watching relationships happen around you doesn't mean you stay an observer. There's a delicate balance between observing life and actively participating with your complete mind, heart and soul. You absolutely must be willing and able to take a stand for your own rights and beliefs, without creating a battle or pressuring others around you to defer, concede or surrender. As I said, it is a delicate balance, an arduous task, but a worthwhile one.

Improve Your Life, One Relationship at a Time

Consider waking up every morning with a clean slate—in a state of unknowing, purposely without any relationship agendas. Each morning, you have the opportunity to redefine and renew your relationship with your partner, and your relationship with the world, and with yourself!

Examples

The value of the principles in this book (and in the world) is in their application, not in just knowledge or understanding alone. Here are some arbitrary but relevant ideas for relationships that could be improved, strengthened or enhanced by applying these principles.

- **Parent/Child**

    The need for honesty to promote trust and intimacy between a parent and a child is profound. Without it, there really is no true bond. Without these elements the parent becomes the disciplinarian, bread-winner, or spiritual jailer—not roles that any of us want. As mentioned earlier, the relationship between parent and child is unique. Acceptance and support are the foundation of this relationship.

    There are natural boundaries that should not be violated between parent and child. These include inappropriate sharing of feelings and problems that would confuse, distress or threaten the child. Given that, I think that it is beneficial for children to be aware of their parent's internal struggles and experiences when they reach an age of understanding and have their own personal strength and belief system, and subsequently, their own struggles..

- **Child/Parent**

    For us who are fortunate enough to have our parent(s) around, there is a great opportunity to improve our relationship with them. Do you feel like you can have more intimate conversations with a parent? Are there happy memories for discussion that could open hearts? I suggest that you need to proceed gently and carefully. These relationships are generally already defined by years of habit and mental patterning. Introducing new dynamics and concepts could shake things up quite a bit. So, remember, easy does it!

- **Extended Family**

    We've all heard or experienced horror stories about conflicts within the extended family. All those "mother-in-law" jokes do have some basis in reality. Can these be improved? Absolutely! The vital requirement here is to accept those family members for who they are. And, when all else fails, be grateful that at least they don't live with you! Unless they do, in which case your situation might very well be hopeless! Edsel says "sorry!".

- **Friends**

  I have found that the most profound application of these intimacy principles is with friends. Our relationships become deeper, more trusting, and take on dimensions and depth that they've never had before. Sharing thoughts, actions or feelings honestly and respectfully are the stuff that makes these friendships really meaningful. To be known to your friends as being genuine is a tremendous gift. The world demands compliance and deferment. Real friends demand nothing but honesty and loyalty.

- **Strangers**

  Yes, I'm talking about the guy standing next to you in the elevator, the lady who runs the coffee concession, and the cashier at the supermarket. For a brief time, we have a relationship with each individual, though fleeting. Imagine the value these strangers would feel if you appropriately shared a little part of your self with them. You could easily brighten their day and make them feel like an important part of your life. Again, what a gift this is! For them, and for you.

We have totally different genetic backgrounds, different life experiences, and even opposite political views! So what is it that we have in common?

Honesty and commitment! With that, we're a perfect match...so give us a kiss!

Chapter 14

Intimacy in Review

Major points to remember in your journey of love and intimacy.

Applying these principles is an exercise in diligence and mindfulness, leading to opportunities for improvement and increased trust and comfort with those around you. Meanwhile, here is a review of the principles of intimacy that we have discussed.

Review—Principles of Maintenance

- o   Abide by the 24-Hour Rule
- o   Share honestly, even when it hurts!
- o   Change patterns of physical interaction often. Even if the habit is working, change it anyway.
- o   Share ideas and fantasies freely and openly. Be willing to discuss the feelings of insecurity and threats that this poses.
- o   Be willing to accept that your partner is not the "be all, and end all." Understand and accept that it is impossible for one single person to satisfy all of your needs and desires.
- o   Celebrate differences.
- o   Work at being wrong! This author is an expert!
- o   If you have developed a pattern of dishonesty in the relationship—experiment with honesty with someone else (not another potential lover, please). Get suggestions on the proper pace and extent of correction and renewed honesty.
- o   Stop comparing your relationship to other people's, or to those in the media. There is no relevancy!

- o Continue to make love, even through periods of stress and discomfort. Pierce the transitory feelings.
- o If you feel that you are being "captured" or your autonomy and/or "self" is being compromised, be willing to share this with your partner. Be prepared for defensiveness and some contention, but always get back to expressing the feelings, not defending or justifying them!
- o Consider establishing rituals within your daily routine with your partner. These tend to create continuity and comfort even through dry periods. This is critical (there is go again)!
- o Eliminate lies and deception from your intimate relationship, and even relationships in general. Understand, and apply that any lie (even by omission) will weaken your foundation, and undermine your intimacy. Truth might appear to strain a relationship, but lies make it meaningless and empty. There is no exception to this!
- o Whenever possible (and appropriate), engage in public displays of affection. Similar to making marriage vows public, these experiences tend to endorse and reinforce the bond of the relationship. And greatly distracts and entertains passer-bys!
- o Don't confuse values and commitment with transient feelings. Feelings are fluid, but the relationships require integrity and loyalty.
- o When you're happy, laugh! And when you're sad, cry! Share *all* with your partner!
- o Play with your partner often.

Finally, if you are stuck within yourself and unclear as to the next step, remember **Rule 62:** Don't take yourself and everything else so damned seriously.

Many of us tend to overanalyze, overreact, create dramas and try to control circumstances and other people. As a result, we scare ourselves, and end up feeling trapped and suffocated. Rule 62 to the rescue—surrender to the humor of it all.

Afterglow

In Chapter One, I shared an intimate story of my wake-up call to authenticity. Such a call shakes the foundations of reality as we know it, and it takes great courage and persistence to respond to that new awareness. Yet, I did respond and life took on new dimensions, relationships and levels of intimacy.

I've shared what I've learned about this intimacy journey throughout the subsequent chapters. In chapter two the discussion focused on the places and spaces in relationships where we are asleep or unaware. To step into a new journey requires realizing that you make mistakes, and then being willing to change them, or even not. Obviously we have to identify mistakes in order to change mistakes, right?

Answering the Call

People often believe that a wake-up call or an "Ah-ha moment" is about suddenly seeing truth. Far from it! More likely, these sudden insights allow you to see what "not truth" is. You see the illusions and delusions, and typically, get confused and frustrated. This step in the process is worthy of celebration, and eventually can lead to clarity.

We discover that our intimacy scripts are often based on media-induced myths and other stories. We learn that all of our feelings are real, but they don't necessarily mean we are in love. The challenge is to discern the meaning of our emotions clearly from our own inner truths, and separate reality from any scripts that play in our head.

Not Surrendering

The deeper message underlying relationship scripts is that you have to earn your way by giving up a part of yourself. Not true!

Knowing we are whole within ourselves, as is our partner, leads us to the awareness that no two human beings will completely satisfy each other. In spite of what you have seen in the movies, or heard in songs, it just doesn't happen. Our seeking satisfaction is at the root of our constant dissatisfaction.

Rather than your partner being the essential ingredient for your happiness, I submit that separateness, acceptance, empathy and respect are the essential ingredients for intimacy.

Being intimate with another also requires that you are aware of your own fears and insecurities. This way you can be honest with your partner, share these doubts and fears, and find acceptance within your intimate's heart.

In the midst of spiritual repression, an external event like my own wakeup call is effective in jarring loose the framework and rattling the bars screaming for freedom.

Freedom is climbing onto the eagle's back, taking magical flight and rising higher to gain perspective on your life. Freedom is respecting constant differences and fluidity that make relationships vital and meaningful. Freedom is the ability and willingness to see the untruths, accept them, and make a choice for change.

Committed Relationships

Our emotional memories keep us from making a real commitment in a relationship. We conjure up the "ghostly" great-feeling memories of first falling in love, and when those feelings aren't present 24-hours a day, we convince ourselves that love is all wrong and the relationship doomed. We all do that. It is like a mass hysterical reaction to soap operas.

So it naturally follows that when your partner is no longer in the defined role in which you found them or learned to appreciate them, or when reality takes the place of the early flighty feelings of adoration and completeness, you feel deceived, and even cheated and believe that love may be gone.

Commitment in itself does not solve this problem. It eliminates it.

The Closed System

An inherent weakness in the totally monogamous relationship is the inability or threat posed by going outside of that relationship to get certain needs met. Not specifically physical needs, but more likely intellectual and spiritual needs. So, when you're thinking that your partner is not fulfilling all of your needs, you can blame him, or take responsibility.

How do you handle the "I don't feel the same about you any more" dilemma? My solution is not to point fingers at others. Wait several days (or seconds), and the feelings will change again. Your perception may shift. And open, honest dialogue brings the feelings to the forefront in a safe, supportive environment.

If it persists, it may be time to realize that there will always be times when you need another advocate other than your intimate, and you may find another safe advocate outside your intimate relationship. But, again, this needs to be done honestly and openly. Sneaking into these other relationships is the foundation for failure, and is truly a violation of the primary relationship. It is a lie. And lies always destroy relationships.

You Can Only Evolve

In mature relationships, intimacy is all or nothing. I make this statement boldly.

Beware! Freedom is addictive. Once you taste it within a relationship, once you experience the privilege of being yourself in an evolving relationship, you will never settle for anything less. We can never choose prisons of love and delusion when open-hearted love and complete acceptance are the alternatives. Even on your darkest day.

Please remember. The mythic relationship images that we have accepted, and their subsequent use as a foundation for real life relationships, keep us miserably frustrated, morbidly disappointed, and undeniably imprisoned. Once you step out of those dramas and traumas, your energy is free to unfold. If being in intimate relationships is a learning experience, then work at diligently at evolving as an individual.

Change and Diversity

Throughout this book I've challenged the roles that capture us and drive us to capture others, and ourselves. What we are learning to do is acknowledge them, define them, limit them, and play with them. My invitation to you is to accept that you are whole and perfect. And a truly intimate relationship makes you more so.

The real dance of intimacy is the music called change and diversity. Intimacy comes from your attitude and willingness, and from your shared experiences. Honesty contributes highly to relationship longevity.

The constant theme of a good relationship is the professed and honored commitment between the partners. The dynamic of true intimacy is one of mutual exposure, disclosure, empathy, honesty, and finally, acceptance. Be forewarned, though. Acceptance does not eliminate conflict, or pain. It allows and honors it.

If you are honest about your feelings, and you can be intimate and share them with your partner, you have done your job and met your responsibility in the relationship. In an intimate partnership, the trust between you and your lover creates a safe network for communication and acceptance. Each must be able to say anything, even if it sounds like nonsense or is lacking in reason. Verbalizations need to be viewed as only partial tools of communication. Ideas, concepts and even feelings that are presented very rarely represent all that is there . . . it is only a small glimpse of the whole. If you remember this, words themselves, though sometimes harsh, are understood to be non-threatening, and even acceptable.

Tension!

What you value is the foundation for intimate relationships; so sorting through and defining your values is critical. You are the only one who speaks for you. Engage the tension. To yourself be true to avoid the capture-surrender games.

When tension in a relationship is supported by your commitment, it can ignite and re-ignite the passion and the joy of your relationship on a daily basis.

The opportunity this book represents is for you to have intimacy without surrender. That means not being captured by profound or even subtle reactions that you have come to identify as the "me".

You only have one choice for true intimacy: To be real, authentic, honest and committed.

I'm glad you woke up. It is nice to have comrades on the road of real intimacy. So share it with others, won't you?

Thanks!

Intimacy
By Edsel Terrick

Light bleeds into darkness,
Claiming space once holy and still,
Boasting triumph . . .
Yet as most battles, one that never needed to be fought.
Sound violates silence.
An absurdly powerful lion shamelessly devours
A princely lamb
Out of fear, when there is no threat.
Substance mocks emptiness, foolishly believing
There is a reason,
When truly . . .
There is none.
Everywhere are meaningless dramas that
Lure the soul and heart
Into a space
Much, much too small.
Answers annihilate questions,
Suffocating them,
Without regard for human dignity
Or personal diversity.
Order imprisons chaos,
Devoid of acceptance and
Capturing possibilities and joy.
The jailer is us.
But sometimes there is a reprieve.
My heart rebels—
And is joined
By you, my fellow conspirator!
Dearest one, be with me.
In my sadness and grief,
In my happiness and joy.
Remind me always that even
When lonely, I am not alone.
And even when feeling unlovable,
I am loved.
We give this gift to one another.
Freely.

CAUTION: Spiritual Anarchy can make you feel different!

Chapter 15

"Now for Something Completely Different"

-Monty Python

Kneel before me. I said… KNEEL! Is not this simpler? Is this not your natural state? It's the unspoken truth of humanity that you crave subjugation. The bright lure of freedom diminishes your life's joy in a mad scramble for power. For identity. You were made to be ruled. In the end, you will always kneel.
German Old Man: [Stands] Not to men like you.
Loki: There are no men like me.
German Old Man: There are always men like you.

-Loki, from "The Avengers", Marvel Cinema

So now that we've viewed, reviewed, considered, analyzed, and discussed the nature and process of relationships, I am hoping that you have come to this spiritual conclusion. Relationships, as what appears to be life itself, is a very elaborate and enticing, but self-created, dream.

I know. This is a harsh statement. But since you have read this far, Edsel Terrick needs to invite you to take this journey of self-discovery, and self-awareness. We STILL are in the realm of relationships, with just one minor shift. We are now considering our relationship with the world, and self.

Happiness and "contentment" themselves are often misunderstood. We are trained early on to seek these experiences and feelings. You have been reading this book most likely with the objective of re-creating or improving your relationship(s) in order the be happy.

This is quite understandable. Truly, all you want is to be happy. All your desires and self-identified "needs", whatever they may be, are longing for happiness.

This is quite understandable. Our minds quickly equate happiness with survival itself. This is a prime directive of self, and the mind is the main tool of the self.

Desire in itself is certainly not wrong. It is a reflection of life itself. It is the urge to grow in knowledge and experience. How, and why, should it be any other way!?

However, it is the choices you make that are wrong, or at least quite self-defeating or even destructive. To imagine that some little thing… like the attention or acceptance by another person, or food, sex, power, or fame will make you happy is to grievously deceive oneself.

Only something as vast and deep as your real self can make you truly and lastingly happy. Edsel Terrickly speaking, happiness is ALREADY THERE! It is your belief that it has to be labeled, chased, captured, and kept that is the actual cause of not experiencing it! Yes, certainly a paradox. But consider this for your own life.

Yes. Another Edsel Terrick Story…

Years ago, whilst living in New York City, I had a quite interesting experience (actually, I had many. This is but one!).

I used to work out at Gold's Gym. Loved it. I would go every couple of days and really enjoy the experience of feeling and moving my body. And learning to strengthen muscles, and feel the joy of moving.

Well, as you might surmise, I was not especially social. I was there to exercise and enjoy. Not to make friends.

But one morning, while sitting in the locker room, I was "cornered" by a fellow member. He got me trapped in the locker room… no way out! So, devoid of my encouragement, he proceeded to share with me his dilemma.

He started out by remarking that I always looked "happy". He wanted to know why. Of course, being Edsel Terrick, I replied by explaining to him that I was happy merely due to the fact that I had no reason not to be.

Well, this went way over his head. And he felt sufficiently motivated to present his problem to me.

He was struggling with the strong need to be happy. Or, more accurately, experience happiness as a happening, rather than as a natural condition.

He had come to the conclusion that if he only had a million dollars, he would be happy. That was it. Simple. And easy to aim at.

I was intrigued (or, at least, amused). I asked him if anything else in his life gave him the pleasure, or satisfaction, that he was seeking. Of course, his answer was a resounding "no".

It was a million dollars, or nothing.

I wished him well. And got dressed and left in short order. That could have been the end of it. But there was more for me to learn…

About three months later. Same gym, same locker rooms, same fellow member. He looked even more sorrowful and discouraged than before!

My curiosity over-road my good sense. I proceeded to inquire about his journey towards ultimate happiness and bliss. The news was even worse than expected…

He had MADE the million dollars! It was in the bank. All safe and secure. But (you KNEW there was a "but" here) he was still not happy. Actually, he seemed even more despondent than before.

So what happened? Well, he made the million, and felt a wave of satisfaction and happiness. But then realized that he had inadvertently misplaced the decimal point. It was TEN million he needed. Not a mere one million.

Yes. A true story. YIPES!

Who You Are, and Who You're NOT

You are constantly making one small error. The mind, and it's very thoughts and feelings, are NOT you. They are created. With great veracity… yes. But merely created. They are not who you are.

You take these creations and imaginings to be real, and a reflection of who you are, and how intimacy itself is to be expressed and experienced. It is not.

You believe the world to be objective, while it is entirely a projection of your mind, and subsequent invented desires.

This is your last chance. After this, there is no turning back. You take the blue pill – the story ends, you wake up in your bed and believe whatever you want to believe. You take the red pill – you stay in Wonderland and I show you how deep the rabbit-hole goes.

-Morpheus, from "The Matrix"

This is NOT bad news. On the contrary, this is wonderful news. No longer do you need to be trapped by the delusions and demands of the people of in this world. Even more importantly, you don't have to be imprisoned and misdirected from the patterns and ramblings of your own thoughts and beliefs.

Instead of continually buying new furniture for the old house, or re-arranging it, you can tear down the house! Ridiculously and radically inspiring.

In other words (OH, there are SO many words!) the gauge the we customarily use to judge the value of relationships, and different aspects of our lives, is faulty. It does not measure what is really important. Mostly because what it DOES measure is of little or no importance. Just another distraction in a whole line of, sometimes amusing, but mostly terrifying distractions and projections.

> *Once you realize that the road is the goal and that you are always on the road, not to reach a goal, but to enjoy its beauty and its wisdom, life ceases to be a task and becomes natural and simple, in itself an ecstasy.*
>
> -Nisargadatta Mahara

Meditation. The Experiencing of Reality

I know what you're thinking (or not!). Why all of these quotes? Appropriate and understandable question.

The answer is that the principles and practices that I am referring to in this chapter are NOT of my discovery, or realization. These are principles that have been recorded and handed down for millennium, if not longer. And that's quite a long time, even to a dinosaur such as myself.

Meditation is as old as humanity, or maybe even older! It's an ancient spiritual practice probably dating back to humans sitting silently around a camp fire and contemplating their existence. It has been duly formalized and structured by Indian religions like Hinduism and Buddhism.

It has been adopted as a spiritual practice by Christians and Muslims and now in the modern world mindfulness and meditation are being practiced everywhere from schools to businesses to the military.

However, it is vitally important to understand that meditation is NOT merely coaxed distraction, or a periodic change of focus. To be effective, it needs to be understood, and applied, rigorously (but gently).

To put it quite simply, meditation is the awareness of life itself, in its inconsistency, confusion, pleasure, pain, disappointment, and sorrow. And the realization that life itself is inside of each of us. Not in our thoughts, beliefs, or color of underwear, but as a part of a greater unity. I know... NO CLUE! Yes, that's the point!

> *No, I don't know where I'm goin'*
> *But I sure know where I've been*
> *Hanging on the promises in songs of yesterday*
> *And I've made up my mind*
> *I ain't wasting no more time*
> *Though I keep searchin' for an answer*
> *I never seem to find what I'm lookin' for*
> *Oh Lord, I pray you give me strength to carry on*
> *'Cause I know what it means*
> *To walk along the lonely street of dreams*
> *And here I go again on my own*
> *Goin' down the only road I've ever known*
> *Like a drifter, I was born to walk alone*
> *And I've made up my mind*
> *I ain't wasting no more time*
> *Just another heart in need of rescue*
> *Waiting on love's sweet charity*
> *I'm gonna hold on for the rest of my days*
> *'Cause I know what it means*
> *To walk along the lonely street of dreams*
>
> *And here I go again on my own*
>
> -Whitesnake

To Be Truly Empowered...

This book is written to make your life better. I understand that you believe that if you would just find your Mister or Mrs. Wonderful it would "solve your problems". But, please, follow this. Your lack of a partner, or attachment to one that seems to be non-gratifying or disappointing, is in fact not the problem. So your solution is ineffective. Even on a good day!

If there IS a problem, it emanates from you. Since you created it (and are constantly doing so) you are the only one who can solve it. Or, better yet, realize that there IS no problem. Just a bundle of desires, memories, projections, fears, anticipations, and empty dreams.

Yuck! That's hard to swallow. Better to be a worn out Greyhound chasing a metal rabbit? Realizing the rabbit is not even worth chasing! It was never as delicious as you thought it was. And can actually break your teeth! If, of course, you ever catch it.

So, as a final admonition from yours truly, Edsel Terrick.

STOP.

"Be still, and know that I am God"

-God

Riders on the storm
Riders on the storm
Into this house we're born
Into this world we're thrown
Like a dog without a bone
An actor out on loan
Riders on the storm

There's a killer on the road
His brain is squirmin' like a toad
Take a long holiday
Let your children play
If ya give this man a ride
Sweet family will die
Killer on the road, yeah

Girl ya gotta love your man
Girl ya gotta love your man
Take him by the hand

Make him understand
The world on you depends
Our life will never end
Gotta love your man, yeah

Riders on the storm
Riders on the storm
Into this house we're born
Into this world we're thrown
Like a dog without a bone
An actor out on loan

Riders on the storm
Riders on the storm

-Jim Morrison, The Doors

That's all Folks!
-Edsel Terrick

I want to be like you
when I grow up!

Don't be like me, be
like YOU when you
grow up.

ABOUT THE AUTHOR

Edsel Terrick

Biography

With an earned doctorate in the knocks of life, Terrick offers his credentials to all the other "slow learners" out there who may identify with him as they read about his outrageous journeys. What makes his story especially unique are the confessed "detours" in life: dependence on drugs and alcohol and subsequent recovery over 35 years ago, one "failed" marriage and one "terminated" marriage. Edsel's beautiful Thai wife, Keaw, and he characterize and maintain their relationship with a level of honesty, trust, and communication that he never thought possible. Terrick has served as his own laboratory for the principles and concepts presented in this book. And, they work! So he thought, "Hey, I ought to write a book about this."

Edsel's formal education consists of a Master of Education in counseling from the University of Massachusetts and the subsequent licensing to practice psychotherapy and family counseling. He published a number of articles in *Professional Counselor Magazine* during in the 1980s and 1990s and continues to do intervention and co-dependency work.

Much of life is acknowledging what is and taking responsibility to either embrace it or change it. At age thirty-four, Edsel owned up to being 275 pounds with a body-fat ratio of over forty percent. Combined with hypoglycemia, bronchial asthma, lack of education regarding proper nutritional principles and the need for physical activity, his body was screaming for attention. The situation mandated that Edsel start "walking the walk" and stop "gulping the cheeseburgers."

As a result of his personal experiences and further education in fitness and responsible lifestyle choices, he became a sought-after fitness advocate and educator. He is well known in today's fitness world for the combination of practical wisdom and ability to connect the improvement of physical fitness and wellness with spiritual development, wholeness, and ultimately, true personal fulfillment. For three years, he wrote a "Health, Fitness and Lifestyle" weekly column that was syndicated to over a million readers in the northeast.

This book moves Edsel Terrick to the next phase of his work in the world, which is to teach, explain, talk and mentor larger numbers of people about the true principles of intimate relationships and awakening of self.